‖‖ ‖ ‖‖‖ ‖‖‖‖‖‖‖‖‖‖‖‖‖‖‖‖‖‖ ‖‖ ‖‖

✔ KT-171-381

Director	**Max Stafford Clark**
Designer	**Tim Shortall**
Lighting Designer	**Johanna Town**
Sound Designer	**Gareth Fry**
Assistant Director	**Jessica Swale**
Dialect Coaches	**Jean-Pierre Blanchard,**
	Mary Blewitt, Kate Godfrey,
	Gabo Wilson
Production Manager	**Laurence Holderness** (NT)
	Gary Beestone (Out of Joint)
Stage Manager	**David Milling** (NT)
Deputy Stage Manager	**Sharon Hobden** (NT)
Assistant Stage Managers	**Ali Biggs**
	Harry Guthrie (NT)
Costume Supervisor	**Caroline Waterman** (NT)
Associate Sound Designer	**Carolyn Downing**
Assistant to the Designer	**Jason Southgate**
Assistant to Lighting Designer	**Nathan Seabrook**
Design Associate	**Alan Bain**
Assistant Production Manager	**James Manley** (NT)
Production Photographer	**John Haynes**

Setting: Kigali, Rwanda, early 1994

The Overwhelming was originally developed in the US
at Salt Lake Acting Company with support from the
NEA/TCG Theatre Residency Program. The play was
further developed with the support of PlayPenn

Biographies

JUDE AKUWUDIKE
Joseph Gasana

Jude Akuwudike trained at RADA. His work in **theatre** includes *Ion, Richard II, The Machine Wreckers, Not About Nightingales, Honk! The Ugly Duckling, Edmond* and *Henry V* at the National; *Luminosity, Brixton Stories, The Winter's Tale* and *Pericles* for the RSC; *The Relapse* at Birmingham Rep; *The Recruiting Officer, Our Country's Good* and *Marching for Fausa* at the Royal Court; *Young Hamlet* at the Young Vic; *Pericles* and *Man Falling Down* at the Globe; *A Doll's House* for Shared Experience; *Moon on a Rainbow Shawl* at the Almeida, and *The Park* at Sheffield Crucible. His work on **TV** includes *Bad Girls, The Last Detective, A Likeness in Stone, Roger Roger, Between the Lines, The Bill, Sam's Duck, Virtual Murder, Downtown Lagos, Madmen and Specialists* and *Land of Dreams*. **Films** include *A World Apart, Sahara,* and *Whisper the Way of the Child*. **Radio** includes *The No. 1 Ladies' Detective Agency, Tide Race, Jero, Humans and Other Animals, Westway* and *Measure for Measure*.

WILLIAM ARMSTRONG
Charles Woolsey / British Doctor

William Armstrong trained at RADA. His work in **theatre** includes *The Blue Ball, Uncle Vanya, Schweyk in the Second World War, Guys and Dolls* and *The Beggar's Opera* at the National; *King Lear, The Merchant of Venice, The Love Girl and the Innocent, Hamlet* and *Richard III* at the RSC; *Shirley, Road* and *Edmond* at the Royal Court and *Glengarry Glen Ross* at the Donmar. His work in **TV** includes *New Street Law, The Golden Hour, Spooks, Rosemary and Thyme, Murder In Suburbia, Murder Prevention, The Brief, Casualty, Capital City, Waking the Dead, Dalziel and Pascoe, Down to Earth, Without Motive, Sunday, La Vie en Rose, The Vice, Band Of Brothers, RKO 280* and *Silent Witness*. **Films** include *David Kelly, Derailed, Bride of Ice, Carmen, The Point Men, Danny, Champion of the World, Hope and Glory, Superman IV, The American Way* and *The First Modern Olympics*.

BABOU CEESAY
Gérard

Babou Ceesay trained at Oxford School of Drama. His work in **theatre** includes *Macbeth* for Out of Joint on international tour; *The Long Goodbye* at the Cockpit Theatre; *Suddenly Last Summer* and *Trojan Women* at the Studios and *Twelfth Night* at the Pegasus Theatre. His work in **film** includes *Severance* and *Light*. **Radio** includes *Just Joshua, Giles Wembbley Hogg Goes Off, Cartouche, Little Photographer* and *The Dissolution of Dominic Booth*.

CHIPO CHUNG
Rwandan Doctor / Elise Kayitesi

Chipo Chung trained at RADA. Her work in **theatre** includes *Gaudeamus* at the Arcola; *Talking to Terrorists* for Out of Joint and the Royal Court; *The Lunatic Queen* at Riverside Studios; *Tall Phoenix* at Coventry Belgrade; *Ma Rainey's Black Bottom* and *The Mayor of Zalamea* at Liverpool Everyman and *Hamlet* at the Nuffield, Southampton. Her work for **TV** includes *Absolute Power*. **Films** include *Proof* and *Sunshine*. Her work in **radio** includes *Falco* and *Sagila*. She is a founder member of Zimbabwe's Over the Edge theatre company.

NICK FLETCHER
Jean-Claude Buisson/Verbeek

Nick Fletcher trained at Webber Douglas. His work in **theatre** includes *Once in a Lifetime, Playing with Fire* and *The UN Inspector* at the National; *Rattle of a Simple Man, King Lear* and *Star Quality* in the West End; *The Slight Witch* and *Silence* at the Birmingham Rep; *Two Gentlemen of Verona* and *A Midsummer Night's Dream* in Regent's Park; *Henry V* and *A Chaste Maid in Cheapside* at the Globe; *Burdalane* at BAC; *A Wife Without a Smile, The House Amongst the Stars, Court in the Act, The Way of the World, The Last Thrash* and *The Cassilis Engagement* at the Orange Tree; *All's Well That Ends Well* for Chicago Shakespeare Theater; and *Love's Labour's Lost* and *A Difficult Age* for English Touring Theatre. **Films** include *Bring Me the Head of Mavis Davis* and *The Visitor*. **TV** includes *Rough Treatment, After the War* and *Grange Hill*. **Radio** includes *Middlemarch* and *The Death of Chatterton*.

ANDREW GARFIELD
Geoffrey Exley

Andrew Garfield graduated from the Central School of Speech and Drama in 2004. His theatre work includes *Burn, Chatroom* and *Citizenship* at the National; *Mercy* at Soho Theatre; *Kes* and Romeo in *Romeo and Juliet* at the Royal Exchange, Manchester, and *The Laramie Project* and Jamie in *Beautiful Thing* at the Sound Theatre. His work for TV includes the programmes *Swinging, Sugar Rush* and *Caravaggio*; and a short film, *Mumbo Jumbo*. He has also recorded for radio *The Boys Club, Caesar: The Glass Ball Game, The Pelican* and *Church*, all for the BBC. In 2004, he was named Most Promising Newcomer at the Manchester Evening News Awards.

MATTHEW MARSH
Jack Exley

Matthew Marsh's recent work in **theatre** includes *Copenhagen* at the National and in the West End; *The Exonerated* at Riverside Studios; *Conversations After a Burial* at the Almeida; *The Little Foxes* at the Donmar; *Us and Them* at Hampstead Theatre and *A Buyer's Market* at the Bush. Recent **TV** includes *The Commander, Service, Hotel Babylon, Surviving Disaster, Belonging, Return of the Dancing Master* and *Wall of Silence*. His recent **films** include *An American Haunting, Land of the Blind, O Jerusalem, Bad Company, Miranda, Quicksand* and *Spygame*.

TANYA MOODIE
Linda White-Keeler

Tanya Moodie trained at RADA. Her work in **theatre** includes *The Darker Face of the Earth* and *The Oedipus Plays* at the National; *Trade, The Prince of Homburg, The School for Scandal, Peer Gynt, Coriolanus* and *Measure for Measure* at the RSC; *Lysistrata* at the Arcola; *Fewer Emergencies* and *Incomplete and Random Acts of Kindness* at the Royal Court; *The Vagina Monologues* in the West End; *A Doll's House, Medea and As You Like It* at West Yorkshire Playhouse; *Much Ado About Nothing* at Salisbury Playhouse; *Anything Goes* for Grange Park Opera and *The Piano Lesson* at the Tricycle. Her work in **TV** includes *Archangel, Shane, Absolute Power, Prime Suspect, Promoted to Glory, In Deep, High Stakes, Holby City, Always and Everyone, The Bill, Dr Willoughby, Maisie Raine, Boyz Unlimited, A Respectable Trade, Neverwhere, So Haunt Me* and *The Man from Auntie*. **Films** include *Rabbit Fever, The Tulse Luper Suitcases* and *The Final Passage*. **Radio** includes *Passing* and *With Great Pleasure*.

LUCIAN MSAMATI
Rwandan Politician/Policeman/ UN Major

Lucian Msamati's work in **theatre** includes *The President of an Empty Room* and *Mourning Becomes Electra* at the National; *ID* at the Almeida; *Who Killed Mr Drum?* at Riverside Studios; *The Firework-Maker's Daughter* at the Lyric Hammersmith; *Fabulation, Gem of the Ocean* and *Walk Hard* at the Tricycle; *Romeo and Juliet* at the Dancehouse, Manchester; *The Taming of the Shrew* at Bath Shakespeare Festival, which he also directed, and international productions of *Born African, Twelfth Night, Fade to Black, Eternal Peace Asylum, Loot, Urfaust* and *A Midsummer Night's Dream*. His work on **TV** includes *Spooks, Ultimate Force, Too Close for Comfort* and *The Knock*. **Films** include *Short Cuts, Coffin, Dr Juju* and *Lumumba*. **Radio** includes *Colours*. He is a founder member of Zimbabwe's acclaimed Over the Edge theatre company.

ADURA ONASHILE
Woman in Club

Adura Onashile's work in **theatre** includes *Macbeth* for Out of Joint; *A Midsummer Night's Dream* at the Pegasus Theatre; *Black President* at the Barbican; *Trek* at the Young Vic; *Hippity Hop* at the Lyric Hammersmith; *The Red Ladies* for the Clod Ensemble; *Cyberschwartze 2* at the Oval House Theatre and productions of *Cleanliness Is Next To Godliness, Hello from Bertha* and *Trojan Women*.

DANNY SAPANI
Samuel Mizinga

Danny Sapani's work in **theatre** includes *His Dark Materials, Antony and Cleopatra, The Machine Wreckers* and *Richard II* at the National; *Julius Caesar*

at the Globe; the title role in *Macbeth* for Out of Joint's national and international tour; *To The Green Fields Beyond* at the Donmar; *Neverland* at the Royal Court; *Measure for Measure* at Nottingham Playhouse; the title role in *Othello* at The Byre, St Andrews; *Measure for Measure* for Cheek by Jowl; *The Lion* for Talawa; *Love at a Loss* for Wild Iris; *The Honest Whore* at the Boulevard Theatre and *The Silver Lake* for Wilton's Music Hall. His work on **TV** includes *Blue Murder, Little Britain, Holby City, Serious and Organised, In Deep, Ultimate Force, Fish, Trial and Retribution, Shakespeare Shorts, Casualty, Richard II, Stick with Me Kid, Between the Lines, The Bill* and *B&B Henry*. **Films** include *Song for a Raggy Boy, Anansi, Timecode II* and *Going Down the Road*.

JT ROGERS
Writer

JT Rogers makes his UK debut with *The Overwhelming*. Other plays include *Madagascar* (Pinter Review Prize for Drama; American Theatre Critics Association's best play award), *Seeing the Elephant* (Kesselring Prize nominee for best new American play), and *White People* (finalist for play of the year, LA Drama Critics Circle). In America, his works have been produced by The Next Stage, Epic Rep and SPF (all in NYC); and at the Philadelphia Theatre Company, New Theatre of Miami and the Salt Lake Acting Company of Utah, where he was a 2004-2005 NEA/TCG playwright in residence. JT Rogers has been an artist in residence at the Eugene O'Neill Theater Center and the Edward Albee Foundation, and is recipient of a playwriting fellowship from the New York Foundation for the Arts. He lives in Brooklyn.

MAX STAFFORD-CLARK
Director
Educated at Trinity College, Dublin, Max Stafford-Clark founded Joint Stock Theatre group in 1974 following his Artistic Directorship of the Traverse Theatre, Edinburgh. From 1979 to 1993 he was Artistic Director of the Royal Court. In 1993 he founded Out of Joint. His work as a director has been overwhelmingly with new writing, and he has commissioned and directed first productions by many of the country's leading writers.

TIM SHORTALL
Designer
Tim Shortall's designs for theatre include *The Philanthropist* at the Donmar; *Telstar* at the New Ambassadors; *Elton John's Glasses* at the Queen's Theatre; *900 Oneonta* at the Old Vic and the Ambassadors; *Body and Soul* and *The Big Knife* (costume) at the Albery; *Murder by Misadventure* at the Vaudeville and Whitehall; *Two Boys in a Bed* and *Twilight of the Golds* at the Arts; *A Cook's Tour* at Shaftesbury; *Excuses* at Soho Theatre; *Disappeared* at the Royal Court; *Eugene Onegin* and *What You Get and What You Expect* at the Lyric Hammersmith; *Jeffrey* at Greenwich; *The Colonel Bird* at the Gate; *Amen Corner* at the Tricycle; *Singular Women* at the King's Head; *Dead Funny* at Chichester; *See How They Run* at the Theatre Royal Plymouth; *Having a Ball* at Birmingham Rep; *Roots* at Watford Palace Theatre, for which he was nominated for best design at the Barclays TMA Awards; *The Circle* for Oxford Stage Company and *Single Spies* for Theatre Royal Bath and on tour. Designs for dance include new works for the Royal Ballet, Sadler's Wells, Nederlands Dans Theater, Scottish Ballet, Ontario Ballet

Theatre, Dutch National Ballet and Norwegian National Ballet. Designs for TV include *The Nightingale* (RAI prize) and *20th Century Blues*.

JOHANNA TOWN
Lighting Designer
Johanna Town's work in theatre includes *The Permanent Way* (also UK and Australian tours) and *Our Lady of Sligo,* both for the National with Out of Joint; *Rose* at the National and on Broadway; *Six Degrees of Separation* and *All The Ordinary Angels* at the Royal Exchange; *The Dumb Waiter* at Oxford Playhouse; *Dead Funny* at West Yorkshire Playhouse; *Guantanamo* on Broadway, in the West End and at the Tricycle; *ID* at the Almeida and on TV; *Feelgood* (an Out of Joint co-production) and *Little Malcolm and His Struggle against the Eunuchs* at Hampstead and in the West End; *Beautiful Thing* at the Donmar and West End; *My Name is Rachel Corrie* at the Royal Court and West End; *Live Like Pigs* for Guildhall and the Royal Court 50; *Via Dolorosa* and *Top Girls* in the West End; *Arabian Nights* in New York; *O Go My Man* and *Talking to Terrorists* with Out of Joint at the Royal Court; *Shopping and Fucking* (Out of Joint/Royal Court) in the West End and on world tour; *The Steward of Christendom* at the Royal Court, the Brooklyn Academy of Music and Sydney Festival, and *Macbeth,* both for Out of Joint; *The Winterling* at the Royal Court, and *Justifying War* at the Tricycle. She has worked on numerous other productions for Out of Joint and also for the Royal Court where she has been Head of Lighting since 1990.

GARETH FRY
Sound Designer
Gareth Fry trained at the Central School of Speech and Drama in

theatre design. His recent work as a sound designer and occasionally as a composer includes *Theatre of Blood, Fix Up, Iphigenia at Aulis, The Three Sisters, Ivanov* and *The Oresteia* at the National; *Noise of Time* (with the Emerson String Quartet), *Strange Poetry* (with the LA Philharmonic Orchestra), *Mnemonic* (as associate) and *Genoa 01*, all for Complicite; *O Go My Man, Talking to Terrorists* and *Macbeth* for Out of Joint; *Harvest, Forty Winks, Under the Whaleback, Night Songs, Face to the Wall, Redundant, Mountain Language, Ashes to Ashes* and *The Country* at the Royal Court; *The Romans in Britain* at Sheffield Crucible; *The Bull* and *Giselle* for Fabulous Beast Dance Theatre; *Cost of Living* for DV8 at Tate Modern; *Phaedra's Love* at Bristol Old Vic and the Barbican; *Astronaut* for Theatre O; *Zero Degrees and Drifting* for Unlimited Theatre; *Almost Blue* at

Riverside Studios (Associate Director). He also designs the music and sound systems for Somerset House's ice rink.

JESSICA SWALE
Assistant Director
Jessica is currently completing her MA in Directing (Advanced Theatre Practice) at Central School of Speech and Drama, having previously gained a Drama Honours Degree from the University of Exeter. Previous directing credits include *Cigarettes and Chocolate, Animal Farm, Be My Baby, Anansi, 4.48 Psychosis, Amy's View, Twelfth Night, A Midsummer Night's Dream, The Glass Menagerie* and various devised plays. Engagements as Assistant Director include *As You Like It* at the Northcott Theatre, Exeter and *The Ballad of Elizabeth Sulky Mouth* at Greenwich Theatre.

ABOUT THE SURVIVORS FUND

Survivors Fund (SURF) works to improve the lives of the Rwandan Survivors of Genocide. While the genocide destroyed victims by inflicting excruciating physical pain and terrifying mental abuse, the goal of SURF is to rebuild a sense of self and trust in humanity.

SURF celebrates its 10th anniversary next year and hopes to extend its campaign to further raise awareness of the Rwandan genocide, and the plight of survivors today. The campaign will also serve to help raise funds to help SURF continue its work to support widows and orphans of the genocide through its grassroots partners in the UK.

SURF is also focusing its efforts on establishing a Testimony and Educational Resource Centre in Rwanda.

For more information go to www.survivors-fund.org.uk.

The Overwhelming

First performance
Cottesloe Theatre
9 May 2006
before touring with Out of Joint to

Oxford Playhouse
5–9 September
01865 305305   www.oxfordplayhouse.com

West Yorkshire Playhouse, Leeds
12–16 September
0113 213 7700   www.wyp.org.uk

Nuffield Theatre, Southampton
19–23 September
023 8067 1771   www.nuffieldtheatre.co.uk.

Liverpool Everyman
26–30 September
0151 709 4776   www.everymanplayhouse.com

Library Theatre, Manchester
3–7 October
0161 236 7110   www.librarytheatre.com

OUT OF JOINT

outof joint

Out of Joint is a national and international touring theatre company dedicated to the developments and production of new writing. Under the direction of Max Stafford-Clark the company has premiered plays from leading writers including David Hare, Caryl Churchill, Mark Ravenhill, Alistair Beaton, Sebastian Barry and Timberlake Wertenbaker, as well as first-time writers such as Simon Bennett and Stella Feehily.

'You expect something special from the touring company Out of Joint ... here's to their next ten years' **The Times 2004**

Touring all over the UK, Out of Joint frequently performs at and co-produces with key venues such as the Royal Court and the National Theatre. The company has performed in six continents – most recently a world tour of its award-winning, Africa-inspired *Macbeth*. Back home, Out of Joint also pursues an extensive education programme.

'Max Stafford-Clark's excellent Out of Joint company' **The Independent 2004**

Out of Joint's next project is a co-production with Hampstead Theatre: *King of Hearts* by Alistair Beaton, writer of Out of Joint's hit West End comedy *Feelgood* and Channel 4's award-winning David Blunkett satire *A Very Social Secretary*.

'Out of Joint is out of this world' **Boston Globe 2005**

PRODUCTIONS TO DATE

2006 *O go my Man* by Stella Feehily **2005** *Talking to Terrorists* by Robin Soans **2004** *Macbeth* by William Shakespeare; *Sisters, Such Devoted Sisters* by Russell Barr **2003** *The Permanent Way* by David Hare; *Duck* by Stella Feehily **2002** *A Laughing Matter* by April De Angelis & *She Stoops to Conquer* by Oliver Goldsmith; *Hinterland* by Sebastian Barry **2001** *Sliding with Suzanne* by Judy Upton; *Feelgood* by Alistair Beaton **2000** *Rita, Sue and Bob Too* by Andrea Dunbar & *A State Affair* by Robin Soans **1999** *Some Explicit Polaroids* by Mark Ravenhill; *Drummers* by Simon Bennett **1998** *Our Country's Good* by Timberlake Wertenbaker; *Our Lady of Sligo* by Sebastian Barry **1997** *Blue Heart* by Caryl Churchill; *The Positive Hour* by April De Angelis **1996** *Shopping and Fucking* by Mark Ravenhill **1995** *The Steward of Christendom* by Sebastian Barry; *Three Sisters* by Anton Chekhov & *The Break of Day* by Timberlake Wertenbaker **1994** *The Man of Mode* by George Etherege & *The Libertine* by Stephen Jeffreys; *The Queen and I* by Sue Townsend & *Road* by Jim Cartwright

The Company

Director	**Max Stafford-Clark**
Producer	**Graham Cowley**
Marketing Manager	**Jonathan Bradfield**
Administrator and	
Education Manager	**Natasha Ockrent**
Assistant Director and	
PA to Artistic Director	**Naomi Jones**
Literary Manager	**Alex Roberts**
Finance Officer	**Sandra Palumbo**

Board of Directors
Kate Ashfield, Linda Bassett, John Blackmore (Chair), Elyse Dodgson,
Sonia Friedman, Stephen Jeffreys, Paul Jesson, Danny Sapani, Karl Sydow

OjO Education Work
Out of Joint offers a diverse programme of workshops and discussions for
groups coming to see our performances. For full details of our education
programme, resource packs or *Our Country's Good* workshops, contact Max
or Tasha at Out of Joint.

Keep in Touch
For information on our shows, tour details and offers join our free mailing list

Out of Joint

Post:	7 Thane Works, Thane Villas, London N7 7NU
Tel:	020 7609 0207
Fax:	020 7609 0203
Email:	ojo@outofjoint.co.uk
Website:	www.outofjoint.co.uk

Out of Joint is grateful to the following for their support over the years:
Arts Council England, The Foundation for Sport and the Arts, The Baring
Foundation, The Paul Hamlyn Foundation, The Olivier Foundation, The
Peggy Ramsay Foundation, The John S Cohen Foundation, The David Cohen
Charitable Trust, The National Lottery through the Arts
Council of England, The Prudential Awards, Stephen Evans,
Karl Sydow, Harold Stokes and Friends of Theatre, John
Lewis Partnership, Royal Victoria Hall Foundation

Out of Joint is a registered charity 1033059

OJO BOOKSALE We stock many of our current and previous plays at
greatly discounted prices. Please visit www.outofjoint.co.uk

THE NATIONAL THEATRE

The National, founded in 1963, and established on the South Bank in 1976, has three theatres – the Olivier, the Lyttelton and the Cottesloe.

It presents an eclectic mix of new plays and classics, with seven or eight productions in repertory at any one time. It aims constantly to re-energise the great traditions of the British stage and to expand the horizons of audiences and artists alike, and aspires to reflect in its repertoire the diversity of the nation's culture. At its Studio, the National offers a space for research and development for the NT's stages and the theatre as a whole; and through NT Education, tomorrow's audiences are addressed. With its extensive programme of Platform performances, backstage tours, foyer music, exhibitions, and free outdoor entertainment the National recognises that theatre doesn't begin and end with the rise and fall of the curtain. And by touring, it shares its work with audiences in the UK and abroad.

Information: 020 7452 3400
Box Office: 020 7452 3000
National Theatre, South Bank, London SE1 9PX
www.nationaltheatre.org.uk

Registered Charity No: 224223

Chairman of the NT Board **Sir Hayden Phillips**
Director of the National Theatre **Nicholas Hytner**
Executive Director **Nick Starr**

J T Rogers
The Overwhelming

faber and faber

First published in 2006
by Faber and Faber Limited
3 Queen Square, London WC1N 3AU

Typeset by Country Setting, Kingsdown, Kent CT14 8ES
Printed in England by Bookmarque Ltd, Croydon, Surrey

All rights reserved
© J T Rogers, 2006
'Rwanda – Never Again' © Fergal Keane, 2006

The right of J T Rogers to be identified as author
of this work has been asserted in accordance with Section 77
of the Copyright, Designs and Patents Act 1988

All rights whatsoever in this work are strictly reserved.
Applications for permission for any use whatsoever including
performance rights must be made in advance, prior to any
such proposed use, to John Buzzetti, The Gersh Agency,
41 Madison Avenue, 33rd Floor, New York, NY 10010.
No performance may be given unless a licence has first
been obtained

*This book is sold subject to the condition that it shall not,
by way of trade or otherwise, be lent, resold, hired out or
otherwise circulated without the publisher's prior consent
in any form of binding or cover other than that in which
it is published and without a similar condition including
this condition being imposed on the subsequent purchaser*

A CIP record for this book
is available from the British Library

ISBN 0–571–23367–8
ISBN 978–0–571–23367–0

2 4 6 8 10 9 7 5 3 1

For my son
Henry Rogers

Contents

Acknowledgements 7
Author's Notes 9
Characters 11

The Overwhelming 13

Rwanda – 'Never Again' 131
'Just Words' 135

Acknowledgements

I wish to thank the following organisations and people in both the United States and Rwanda who were instrumental in the development of this play, whether through their support, creative input, professional advice or editorial criticism: the NEA/TCG Theatre Residency Program for Playwrights; all of the artists and staff at the Salt Lake Acting Company, especially Nancy Borgenicht, Allen Nevins, David Kirk Chambers, and David Mong; Professor Howard Lehman of the University of Utah; Paul Meshejian and Michele Volansky and everyone at the PlayPenn new play development conference, with special thanks to my cast and director Lucie Tiberghien; David Rogers; Susan Spencer Smith; Dr Eric Helland; Dr Louis Kayitalire; Adelit Rukomangana; and Helen Vesperini and Jean-Pierre Sagahutu.

Here in London, I am grateful to those whose support or creative input has been instrumental in this play's completion: Nicholas Hytner, Tim Levy and everyone at the National Theatre; Out of Joint; Jessica Swale; this remarkable cast of Jude Akuwudike, William Armstrong, Babou Ceesay, Chipo Chung, Nick Fletcher, Andrew Garfield, Matthew Marsh, Tanya Moodie, Lucian Msamati, Adura Onashile, and Danny Sapani; and most emphatically, Max Stafford-Clark.

Finally I wish to express my gratitude to Rebecca Ashley, who has been involved with this play since its inception. Without her counsel and encouragement it simply would not exist.

J T Rogers
May 2006

Author's Notes

The use of an oblique (/) at the beginning or in the middle of a line of dialogue indicates that the next line of dialogue begins at that moment, creating verbal overlap.

A sentence ending with an ellipsis (. . .) indicates that the speaker has trailed off. A sentence ending with a dash (–) indicates that the speaker is cut off in mid-sentence.

French and Kinyarwanda, the two main languages of Rwanda, are spoken throughout the play. Sometimes the audience is to understand what is being said, sometimes not. When the Rwandan characters speak English, they do so with French-African accents.

Scene numbers are only used to delineate a change in location. The play flies along without stopping for breath, each scene shifting into the next without pause.

Cover image

Young prisoner in Gitarama, Rwanda,
accused of genocide

Characters

THE AMERICAN FAMILY

Jack Exley

Geoffrey Exley
his son

Linda White-Keeler
his wife

OTHER FOREIGNERS

Charles Woolsey
US embassy official

Jean-Claude Buisson
French diplomat

British Doctor
for the International Red Cross

Jan Verbeek
a South African NGO worker

UN Major
a Bangladeshi

THE RWANDANS

Joseph Gasana

Elise Kayitesi
his wife

Samuel Mizinga
Rwandan government official

Gérard
the Exley family's servant

Man at French Embassy Party

Rwandan Doctor

Market Woman

Market Man

Policeman

Woman in the Nightclub

Man in the Nightclub

Waiters, waitresses, party guests, hospital orderlies,
French Embassy servant, nightclub patrons

The play is performed with a cast of eleven

Three actors – two white men and one black woman—
play the Exley family

Two white actors play Woolsey / British Doctor
and Buisson / Verbeek respectively

Two black actors play Elise / Rwandan Doctor
and Joseph and all waiters, orderlies and servant

Two black actors play Mizinga and Gérard

One black actor plays the Man at French Embassy Party,
Market Man, Policeman, Man at the Nightclub,
and UN Major

One black actor plays the Market Woman
and Woman at the Nightclub

Party guests, nightclub patrons, people at the market,
and other secondary roles are played by the company

THE OVERWHELMING

Think –
When you speak of our weaknesses,
Also of the dark time
That brought them forth.

Bertolt Brecht, from *To Posterity*

In the late nineteenth century the Belgian King Leopold II launched a campaign to conquer the Congo basin of Africa. Over the following decades, through conquest and then subjugation, millions of Congolese were killed. The word in the Mongo language for this onslaught was 'lokeli', or 'the overwhelming'.

Setting

The play takes place in Kigali, Rwanda, early in 1994.

Act One

ONE

Friday afternoon. A torrential downpour. Two white Americans – Jack, early forties, and Woolsey, a little older – are in a car. Woolsey is driving. Their conversation is interrupted by a deafening crack of thunder. They shout to be heard over the storm.

Woolsey Don't worry! / These are the best roads in Africa!

Jack I'm fine! Really! Thank you!

Woolsey Water's a different story. Don't ever drink from the tap, whatever people tell you. / That goes for teeth-brushing, too. If you didn't boil it or unscrew it, don't drink it!

Jack I know! I've done a lot of travelling!

Woolsey You ever had serious diarrhoea?

Jack . . . I'm not sure!

Woolsey How long you here?

Jack Just the semester!

Woolsey Well, get ready for it! For the next four months, when you fart, you'll fart with fear!

The rain has stopped, almost instantaneously. The sun comes out. Jack looks around as Woolsey stares straight ahead.

Jack God! That's incredible! / I've been all over the world, but that is . . .

15

Woolsey Flick of a switch turns it on, flick of a switch turns it off.

Jack Amazing.

Woolsey Yes, indeed.

They drive for a moment. Then, leaping back in where they left off . . .

Jack Brezhnev!

Woolsey Perfect example!

Jack (*laughing*) God! I'd forgotten / about him, too.

Woolsey Exactly my point. Like it never happened.

Jack Absolutely right.

Woolsey Forty years. / God knows how much money and blood.

Jack Incredible. Just incredible.

Woolsey Berlin Wall's down, what, four years? Already ancient history.

Jack I don't think my son even knows who Brezhnev was.

Woolsey There's no enemy now. We won. And yet I miss those fuckers. No, I do. I'm old school, Jack. I can say 'Do you want to defect?' and 'How much for the entire night?' in ten languages. There's nothing to push against. We're just going through the motions. Four years I've been here, shuffling papers, picking up tourists at the airport. Why? No one can tell me. What are we protecting? No one can tell me. I don't know, Washington doesn't know, you don't know – *do* you know?

Jack You mean –

Woolsey Yeah. Tell me.

Jack I . . . No, I don't –

Woolsey Come on, Jack. Give me a fresh perspective. We're still strangers; we can say anything.

Jack (*laughing*) Two hours in Kigali and you want my thoughts? I teach International Relations / not mind read – What?

Woolsey Exactly. (*off the word* '*What?*') 'International relations.' With whom? Who are we relating with? Four years, I still haven't gotten an answer. You find an answer, you let me know.

Jack You'll be the first.

Woolsey Anything, really. You find out anything interesting. People. Places. Happenings. You let me know first. Will you do that?

Jack Sure I can. I'm just visiting.

Woolsey Me, too.

Jack I just know one person here.

Woolsey That'll change. You like good beer?

Jack Sure.

Woolsey The beer here tastes like piss. Makes you thirsty for Schlitz. God, what I wouldn't give for an ice-cold Schlitz. Let's swing by UNAMIR before we go to the hotel, see if we can score some Ghanaian stuff.

Jack The Ghanaians make good beer?

Woolsey Geniuses with beer. This is a fucked-up continent, but the Ghanaians, they're doing all right. You wanna go by the embassy and check in first?

Jack Why?

Woolsey Why? Why in a country where people are getting assassinated left and right would you want the United States government to know where you are and how to get in touch with you?

Jack But the Accords are . . .

Woolsey What about them?

Jack There's a ceasefire. There's no fighting.

Woolsey And you know this how?

Jack From . . . everywhere! The BBC, / African news sources. The guerrillas agreed to – the RPF laid down their arms. I contacted people at the UN before coming. They *told* me things were . . .

Woolsey Oh, well, 'the BBC' . . . (*off the word* 'UN') Ho ho! Sweet Jesus.

Jack Are you telling me something different? My family's arriving tomorrow –

Woolsey I'm picking them up too. Don't worry. They'll be fine. You'll be fine.

Jack I'm here for research.

Woolsey Good.

Jack I'm just writing a book.

Woolsey Good.

Jack I *wanted* to come here.

Woolsey Sure.

They drive in silence, looking straight ahead. Then:

Oh. And happy New Year.

TWO

A pool of light reveals Joseph, who speaks out to us.

Joseph Dear Jack, I hope this finds you well. I am sorry to report that I will be unable to meet you at the airport. If I had any choice in the matter, you know I would be there to greet you, my friend. But I will see you after the weekend, first thing Monday morning at my office. It was an unexpected surprise to hear that you have changed your plans and are now bringing your family. But it is wise of you to come a day ahead and make sure everything is in order for them. You have always been cautious, Jack. Here you will find this trait very useful. Unfortunately, the housing I arranged is now no longer adequate, but we will find you something else.

Again, I am so sorry to hear about Carol. This must be a very difficult time for your son. As you say, coming here is not Geoffrey's choice, but I know you will take good care of him. I know you are not a praying man, Jack, but please know that I am praying for you. I find myself doing that more often now. God and medicine: how dearly one needs them both in this life.

THREE

Later that day, Woolsey and Jack, glasses of beer in hand, sit at a table by the pool of the Hôtel des Mille Collines. Jack is in mid-enthusiastic speech.

Jack I would love him to have that kind of experience. Like I did when I was his age.

Woolsey So you've been to Africa before?

Jack No, no. Sweden. Semester abroad. But even that gives you a sense of being the foreign, the, the 'other'.

And since then – Look, through my work I've done village-level research in Indonesia, Peru. Had the kind of first-hand encounters where you experience – viscerally – life as the outsider. There's an empathy that comes from that. I want him to have that, while he's still young enough for it to make a difference. Instil a sense of humility and – yes! – of questioning. God! I don't want to raise another American who doesn't question! I see them in my classes: eighteen years old, this sense of entitlement! The scope of what they take for granted!

Woolsey So you want to take things away from him.

Jack No. I mean . . . well . . .

Woolsey Temporarily.

Jack Yes.

Woolsey For his own good.

Jack Exactly.

Woolsey Well, you've come to the right place for that. If the world were flat, this would be the edge. And you chose to – You're obviously having a good time, I don't want to be the / drunken expat who –

Jack No, no! Please. Tell me what you think of this place. Really.

A Waiter enters and replaces the empty bottles with fresh ones.

Woolsey (*to the Waiter*) Tu veux me soûler, de nouveau, huh? [*Trying to get me drunk again, are you?*]

Waiter Mais bien sûr monsieur, à quoi est-ce que je sers sinon? [*But of course, sir, why else am I here?*]

They both laugh, then, as the Waiter walks away:

Woolsey He's dead.

Jack . . . What?

Woolsey (*gestures off toward the Waiter*) His wife was killed last week. Abducted. Raped. Cut up. Someone thought she was an RPF accomplice. They'll come for him. Matter of time.

Jack Who?

Woolsey Well, that's the million-dollar question isn't it?

Jack Why doesn't he –

Woolsey Run? Go to the police? This isn't Sweden, Jack.

Jack . . . How do you know this?

Woolsey I live here.

FOUR

Joseph appears again in his light, speaking to us.

Joseph In late January you will have missed most of the rainy season and you will find the weather beautiful when you arrive. You must take your family to the Nyungwe Forest while you are here. Bring your tourist dollars so you can buy some ugly trinkets you will never use. Speaking of this, would you please bring me two Michael Jordan T-shirts, size small, in black. This will make me a very popular man.

I am amazed sometimes how little I miss from the States. Except the toilet paper. Just kidding. I cannot wait to begin our work together, Jack. What a pleasure it will be, my friend, to share my country with you.

FIVE

A cocktail reception at the French Embassy, the following evening. A Rwandan Waiter and Waitress silently pass food and drink to party guests. Near the back of the room is a well-dressed Rwandan Man, standing alone. Jack and Woolsey stand together, drinks in hand. Nearby, Linda, a black American in her early thirties, is talking to Buisson, thirties, a French government official. With them is Geoffrey, a white American, seventeen. He is less than happy to be here.

Buisson No, I'm positive. I've seen your photo before.

Linda Well, it could be. I'm –

Geoffrey Denim jacket, hair up in a bun?

Buisson Yes!

Geoffrey It's the dust-jacket shot everyone remembers.

Buisson Ah, you are a writer!

Linda I'm impressed you've even seen / one of . . .

Buisson Are you a poet?

Linda No.

Buisson Novels, then?

Linda Not yet.

Buisson This is like a game . . . Histories of – No, no, don't tell me . . . Black America! Histories of Black America!

Geoffrey She does creative non-fiction.

Buisson . . . I'm sorry?

Linda Personal essays. Narratives of self.

Buisson Ah! Like Montaigne!

Linda Yes!

Buisson What was it Nietzsche said? 'Truly, that such a man has written adds to the joy of life.'

Linda I couldn't agree more. Montaigne is without peer.

Buisson I have read everything of his. If one is French – well, if one is French and in my profession, one must.

Geoffrey 'Living on this earth.'

Buisson . . . I'm sorry?

Geoffrey The quote. It's '. . . adds to the joy of living on this earth.' From *Birth of Tragedy*.

Buisson (*pause*) And do you speak German, Geoffrey?

Geoffrey . . . Uh, no.

Buisson So you are correcting me with a translation.

Linda (*trying to save the boy*) Geoffrey's father and I were just telling him, next year at college he should *take* German. That's what Jack / studied in . . .

Buisson (*staring straight at Geoffrey*) You see, this is the hazard of translation. An idea is written down. Another man is drawn to it. His mission, to spread this thought deeper into the world. But there is a difference between having words and understanding their meaning.

Jack (*gesturing for him*) Geoffrey!

Eagerly taking his 'out', Geoffrey mumbles a goodbye under his breath as he heads toward Jack and Woolsey.

Buisson (*turning to Linda*) What is so often missing is context. And as we diplomats know, not having context is a dangerous thing.

Buisson kisses Linda's hand and crosses to the Rwandan Man, as Geoffrey has joined Jack and Woolsey.

Woolsey So what are you, high school? Eleventh? Twelfth?

Geoffrey Twelfth.

Jack (*to Woolsey*) Very good, Chuck!

Linda flags down the Waitress for a refill. Buisson and the Rwandan Man speak together, as Mizinga, another Rwandan Man, in his late thirties and equally well dressed, enters the room.

Woolsey I've got two sons. All grown up now.

Jack Really!

Woolsey Graduated. Jobs. One's already having a baby.

Jack Your work's done then.

Woolsey (*laughs*) My father told me, 'When you pay the down payments on their first mortgages, then you're done.' So, Geoff –

Jack Actually / he prefers –

Geoffrey I can tell him, Dad. (*to Woolsey*) Geoffrey.

Mizinga has joined Buisson and the other Rwandan Man in conversation.

Woolsey You play sports, Geoffrey?

Geoffrey No.

Woolsey Foreign language?

Geoffrey No.

Jack Geoffrey! (*to Woolsey*) He's fantastic at languages. Just like his mother.

Woolsey Really? Linda told me she couldn't speak a word of –

Geoffrey She's not my mother. You know: kinda obvious.

Jack I mean my first wife. Carol.

Woolsey Carol.

Jack Yes, Geoff's – I mean . . . (*to Geoffrey*) Sorry . . . (*to Woolsey*) Geoffrey's / mother.

Woolsey Carol.

Jack Yes.

Woolsey Carol wasn't in your file, Jack.

Jack Oh. Well. She and I . . . divorced years ago.

Geoffrey *Three* years ago.

Jack Well, okay! Who'd like another drink?

As Jack goes to get refills, Linda is approached by Mizinga.

Mizinga (*in French*) Bonsoir, madame, c'est un plaisir de faire votre connaissance. [*Good evening, madam. It's enchanting to make your acquaintance.*]

Linda Forgive me. I don't speak French.

Mizinga (*switching to English*) Ah! You are *noire Americaine*. Forgive *me*. I mistook you for someone else, equally beautiful.

Linda Sorry to disappoint.

Mizinga Samuel Mizinga.

Linda Linda White-Keeler.

Mizinga (*pause*) I'm sorry?

Linda (*a little slowly*) Linda White-Keeler.

Mizinga . . . This is an American name?

Linda My mother's name is White, and my father's –

Mizinga Ah! 'White' *and* 'Keeler'! Of course. You said 'White-Keeler', and I thought –

He draws his thumb across his throat as Woolsey drifts over to them.

Woolsey Linda, Sam's in the government. One of the ones with all his marbles.

Linda Really?

Mizinga Simply serving my country.

Woolsey He's working on the BBTG.

Linda The . . . ?

Woolsey Sorry. (*to Mizinga*) She's fresh off the plane. (*to Linda*) Broad Based Transitional Government. Now that the shooting's stopped.

Mizinga And how is the golf coming, Charles?

Woolsey Same old, same old.

Mizinga Mr Woolsey is famous here for how far he can hack the ball. But his putting (*as he mimes doing so*) is a painful thing.

Woolsey Thank you, Sam. Always good to be loved.

Mizinga We all play with him, of course. After all, what man does not like to win?

Woolsey (*as he moves back toward Geoffrey*) Happy New Year, Sam.

Mizinga And you, Charles.

As Woolsey and Buisson cross paths . . .

Buisson (*extending his hand*) Bonsoir. Vous serez toujours le bienvenu chez nous. [*Good evening. You will always be welcome here.*]

Woolsey (*brushing past*) Great.

Mizinga (*to Linda*) I am told you are a writer.

Linda That got around quick.

Mizinga I confess, reading is my weakness. Balzac is my favourite. I have read most of him.

Linda Really.

Mizinga The sweep of his work. That one man could capture an entire people. Quite magnificent. Perhaps you will write about us.

Linda Yes! That's – I mean, I'm here to . . . Sorry. Half my brain is still in the States. Yesterday I was in two feet of snow and a down parka. I'm still adjusting to being here in paradise. I hope that's not offensive.

Mizinga Yes, terribly offensive. I shall have to have you shot. (*Pause.*) That was a joke.

Linda Ah! When my husband's son and I flew in today, the mountains were –

Mizinga Like the Alps, people say.

Linda Yes!

Mizinga Rwanda is called the Switzerland of Africa. Or perhaps it should be the other way around. I think you will find we are like the Swiss. Organised, efficient. People take orders here very well. This is why it is so important.

Linda What is?

Mizinga That our leaders have the best interest of this country at heart. There are many of us here who are working very hard to make sure this is the case. We cannot afford to go backward.

Jack returns to Woolsey and Geoffrey, drinks in hand.

Woolsey So, Geoffrey, what *do* you do? Twelfth grade, the world wide open.

Geoffrey Study.

Jack Geoffrey's the district champ in extemporaneous speaking. It's where you draw three topics from a hat. You pick one – global warming, race relations – you get five minutes to prepare. Then you try to persuade the judges to your point of view. Geoffrey came in first this year. The entire school district.

Woolsey What did you speak on?

Geoffrey Organic farming.

Woolsey You won with a speech on organic farming?

Geoffrey Yeah.

Woolsey Sort of a Mother Earth good, pesticides bad kind of a thing?

Geoffrey Sure.

Woolsey Your parents and Linda must be very proud.

Geoffrey Thanks.

Woolsey Terse is good. Terse will get you far in life. Look at me. I ask too many questions. I got sent here.

Linda and Mizinga, in mid-conversation.

Linda Essays, about my personal experiences here.

Mizinga To convey this to American readers?

Linda Yes! It's a much larger magazine than those I usually . . . so I'm thrilled. And intimidated.

Mizinga I am sure your work is excellent.

Linda No. Thank you, but what I mean is, being here, for the first time . . . From what I've learned, I have ancestors from the Great Lakes region. They were taken from here, in chains. I'm *from* here.

Mizinga Then you must feel a bond with –

Linda A responsibility. I don't want to be another tourist waxing lyrical about 'Mother Africa'. I want to really see this place. Ask hard questions. Write something that opens eyes and instils an interest. And now I'm hearing myself, and I sound like some / sort of . . .

Mizinga You are being honest. And for that, I thank you. I hope you will allow me to be of service. To your writing.

Linda That would be . . . thank you. Yes.

SIX

Joseph appears again in his light, speaking to us.

Joseph You will find Kigali a clean city. And safe. Even for Linda. This is not a city where your wife will be afraid to be out at night, like Paris or Milwaukee. Now that she is coming, I am eager to meet her. From your letters, she sounds like a handful. And you have always liked your hands very full, Jack. Congratulations.

Forgive me, my friend, for urging you to come at such short notice. But when one has a window, one must open it. Your coming now allows us to help each other. And we must help our friends, Jack. Always.

SEVEN

The end of the party at the French Embassy, many drinks consumed. The Waiter and Waitress as well as the other party guests are gone. Linda, Woolsey, Buisson, Mizinga, and the other well-dressed Rwandan Man are listening to Jack. Geoffrey sits to the side, watching.

Jack History is this all-powerful, irreducible monolith. This is what we're taught.

Mizinga translates into French for the Man, who stands next to him.

Mizinga L'histoire est une chose toute puissante, monolithique. / Voilà ce qu'on nous enseigne. [*We are taught that history is powerful. It is a monolith.*]

Jack A series of events, outside our control. / This torrent, pouring forth, sweeping all of us, inexorably forward.

Mizinga Il dit que nous sommes tous dans les mains du destin. [*He says, we are all in the hands of fate.*]

Woolsey You're saying that's bullshit.

Jack Exactly! Utter bullshit!

Mizinga Mais l'autre / dit c'est n'importe quoi. [*That one says, you are speaking bullshit.*]

Linda We were in Cuzco when Jack got the idea for the book.

Jack This Dutch couple, running our hotel. Younger than us. (*to Linda*) Well, than me.

Linda This was in Peru, up in the mountains. On our honeymoon.

They are 'on', telling the story together, not for the first time.

Jack They'd adopted twelve boys, just the two of them. / Kids from the slums.

Linda They did this on their own. They told us there was no plan. / It just happened.

Jack They saw all these other children, so they started taking donations / from their guests.

Linda From people like us just passing through.

Jack They feed five hundred children daily.

Linda You saw what they were doing, you *had* to get involved.

Jack These people aren't being swept along, they're doing the sweeping.

Linda And this is when Jack . . . (*She gestures to him to 'take it away'.*)

Jack And the question hits me: what's the connection? Between this couple and people all over the world, affecting change – true change – underneath the radar.

Mizinga (*continuing to translate*) Il dit qu'il y a des gens qui, à eux seuls, sont vraiment capables de changer les choses. / Qu'ont-ils en commun? [*He says there are people in the world who truly change things, all on their own. / So how are they connected to each other?*]

Linda When I took Jack's class, he had us all in the palm of his hand. He'd start talking, and I'd just –

Jack In international relations, you find your question by finding the right lens to look through. Then you seek your answers through creating cross-national models of comparative –

Linda Jargon alert!

Jack (*gestures 'thank you' to Linda*) You collect examples. In this case, individuals. That couple in Cuzco, I started with them. Then a tribal chief I interviewed in Borneo, fighting his government over deforestation. One man!

Buisson And the book you are writing, it is about these sort of people?

Jack Exactly! A comparative analysis of grass-roots activists around the world, standing up for what is right. What's the common variable? Personality? Class? Culture? What can we extrapolate from these people who act, even in the face of the impossible?

Man (*in French*) Vous avez beaucoup de chances. Ici on n'a pas ce genre de personne.

Mizinga (*translating*) 'You are fortunate. Here we do not have these sort of people.'

Jack You do! The heart of my book is about a doctor, here in Kigali. I'm here to write about the work he's doing: one man in one hospital, under the radar. People like this are changing history. / This is what I'm . . .

Mizinga (*translating*) Ce livre il s'agit d'un médecin ici à Kigali. [*He is here for a book about a doctor in Kigali.*]

Jack A book about him. About what he and so many others are accomplishing. Not just another footnoted tome that moulds away in a bunch of university libraries, but something that speaks to the world at large. That galvanises the – (*to Mizinga*) Forgive / me, I'm . . .

Mizinga Please. Your passion is invigorating.

Jack People *do* take action.

Mizinga But not every person here who takes action is to be trusted. You must / learn this.

Jack Of course. What I'm saying is that individuals make a difference.

Mizinga This is in America?

Jack No! Everywhere!

Man (*to Mizinga*) Les gens qui peuvent changer l'histoire? Ils sont partout? Je vous en trouverais moi a Butare? [*These people are 'everywhere'? People who can 'change history'? I am to find them in Butare?*]

Jack Look, this isn't just another theoretical humanist argument. There are concrete examples. People we all know. Look at the Philippines! (*Snaps his fingers.*) What's his, what's / his . . .

Linda Benigno Aquino.

Jack (*to her*) This is why I love you. (*to his 'audience'*) Two heart attacks in solitary confinement, exiled to the States, barely able to walk, but still protesting the Marcos regime. Speaking out, setting an example, one man!

Woolsey And they shot him.

Everyone turns and looks at Woolsey.

Aquino finally flew back, he got off the plane in Manila, and they shot him.

Everyone turns and looks at Jack.

Jack (*pause*) Okay, yes. But my point is –

Linda His wife.

Jack Thank you!

Linda Corazon Aquino stepped into her husband's shoes, Marcos fell, she became president.

Jack A housewife! No political experience, training, interest. History crashes down on her head, and what does she do? She acts! The housewife moves the monolith!

Man Mais ici, nous sommes au Rwanda.

Mizinga (*translating*) 'But this is Rwanda.'

Man Nous n'avons pas de Aquino.

Mizinga 'We have no Aquino.'

Man Nous n'avons pas de Mandela ou de Jefferson.

Mizinga 'We have no Mandela or Thomas Jefferson.'

Man Sans les / hommes de cette envergure, l'histoire ne peut pas changer. Ce qui doit arriver arrivera.

Jack (*to the Man*) I'm sorry, I don't / believe we've . . .

Linda Jack, let him finish.

Mizinga (*off Man's 'envergure'*) 'Without men like that history cannot be changed. What is to happen here will happen.'

Jack (*to the Man*) No. I'm sorry, but no. The world is not dictated by *Kaiser Geschichte*. You / have to . . .

Linda Honey / you're –

Jack (*to Linda*) I know! (*back to the Man*) Forgive me. I know I'm your guest but – Look, Mandela, Jefferson: their impact can't be denied. But glorifying a handful of great individuals releases *us* from responsibility. That couple in Cuzco; this doctor here; you, me: *we're* the ones that have to be willing to stand up and make a difference. This is how history moves forward. One pebble redirects the river!

Buisson But what if the river becomes an ocean?

Linda Then you get more pebbles.

Buisson How pretty that sounds, but / it is not a realistic . . .

Linda What's the alternative? 'It's not my problem?' / That's your paradigm for dealing with the world?

Mizinga You must understand, Jack, we are still a nation in shock. *Inkoytanyi* terrorists have invaded this country, slaughtered our citizens. The UN is here now, and things are quiet, but we have been victims of terrible crimes. We are not ready for what you are speaking about.

Linda But the Arusha Accords are / in place, so everything is . . .

Man (*growing agitated*) Ce pays est encore infesté d'espions et de meurtriers. / Les Hutus se battent pour leur survie. Notre pays est au bord de la destruction. Nous sommes des ésclaves de l'histoire. Nous devons faire tout ce qui est en notre pouvoir pour survivre.

Mizinga (*translating*) 'Spies and murderers are still among us. The real Rwandans are fighting for their survival' – I am only translating, you understand – 'We are holding on to our country by our fingernails. We are trapped by our history. / We must do what we can to survive.'

Jack No, no! I'm sorry. But that's completely fatalistic. I'm not saying to stand up isn't hard. Terribly hard. But look at the world. Look at your country! This endless cycle of ethnic killings – the level of bloodshed. You have to go beyond this! The wheel of history pushed forward by your shoulders! For God's sake, what's the alternative?

The Man speaks to Jack in Kinyarwanda, his voice rising. Words hard, sharp.

Man Uratekereza ko har' ikintu twahindura nizi nyenzi zose zishaka gutwara ubutaka bwacu? Kwica abana bacu? Reb' ibyo barigukorera bagenzi bacu b'aBarundi! Amaraso zameneka, mbere yuko undi mwami ategeka iki gihugu! Ingufuz'abahutu zizatuma! Urwanda rutagwa mu maboko y'Abanyamahanga! Tuzuzuz' amaliba n'amaraso yabo hanyuma tuboherez' iwabo muli Ethiopia! Urumva? Tuzabatema bose! Ntabwo tuzongera kub'abaja!
[*You think we can change things here with these filthy cockroaches all around us? Plotting to take our land? Kill our children? Look what they are doing to our brothers and sisters in Burundi! The streets will run with blood before another Tutsi king rules this country! Hutu Power will save Rwanda from these foreign devils! We will fill the rivers with bodies and send them all back to Ethiopia! Do you hear me? We will cut them, everyone! We will not be slaves again!*]

He finishes. Everyone turns to Mizinga.

Mizinga (*with a smile*) He says, 'Welcome to Rwanda.'

EIGHT

Late that night, Geoffrey's hotel room. Geoffrey stands with towel and toothbrush. Jack stands in the doorway. They stare at each other.

Jack Hi.

Geoffrey Hey.

Silence. Then . . .

Jack If you need any help, anytime, with any of your coursework, Linda or I can –

Geoffrey Thanks. I'll let you know.

36

Jack I know this wasn't exactly how you expected to spend the last semester of / your senior year.

Geoffrey Things happen.

They stare at each other.

Jack Yes. They do.

He turns to leave, then turns back.

Do you . . . do you remember when we went to Bali? We took that boat and went to that isolated island?

Geoffrey I was five. Who remembers things from when / they're five?

Jack Right. Of course. Your mother and I, we took you there. For a week we did nothing. The stillness was . . . We stayed in this hut. The three of us. No electricity. We'd fish out of the sea, cook it right on the beach. (*Laughs at the memory.*) You'd eat all of yours, then half of mine. (*Another memory returns.*) 'Your shoulders are down.' You kept saying that to me. 'You're so relaxed, Daddy, your shoulders are down.' You sure you don't . . . ?

Geoffrey is still, watching him.

For your mother and me, it was . . . transforming. To be so removed. Really see yourself. That kind of clarity can change you. Make things different. I want us to have that, Geoffrey. Here. The three of us. I know you and Linda barely . . . It's difficult for her, too. She never expected – You'll see. You'll get to know her. You'll understand why . . . I know you and I haven't spent a lot of . . . I'm so glad you're here.

They stare at each other.

Geoffrey Goodnight, Dad.

*Monday morning, an office at Kigali Central Hospital.
Jack is meeting with a female Rwandan Doctor. An
Orderly is pouring a bottle of Fanta into a glass for Jack.*

Rwandan Doctor And have you found accommodations?

Jack My wife and son and I have been staying at the
Mills Collins. (*to the Orderly*) Merci.

 *Done serving, the Orderly moves away from them and
 stands unmoving.*

Rwandan Doctor How did you come to choose the *Mille
Collines*?

Jack Oh! Thank you. We didn't have time to find a place
here to rent before we came. So I decided, once we got
here, I'd have to go around asking (*haltingly*) 'Excusez
moi, où pourrais-je trouver une maison à louer?' [*Excuse
me, where can I rent a house?*] I inexplicably took
German in graduate school, so that's the extent of my
French.

Rwandan Doctor But you used it.

Jack I used all of it.

Rwandan Doctor And the effort is appreciated.

Jack Well, I'm – we're all thrilled to be here. My God,
the flight in: breathtaking. The hills. So green. Endless.

Rwandan Doctor A thousand hills.

Jack Exactly! That's the phrase in Kinyarwanda to
describe your country, isn't it?

Rwandan Doctor I am impressed.

Jack Well, one should know something about where /
one is . . .

Rwandan Doctor Your country is named for Amerigo
Vespucci, I believe.

Jack Yes.

Rwandan Doctor An Italian.

Jack That's right.

Rwandan Doctor Why don't you speak Italian in
America? I have always wondered this.

Jack Well, he discovered, but he didn't –

Rwandan Doctor But he was there first.

Jack No, Christopher Columbus was first. (*Pause.*) I think.

Rwandan Doctor Christopher Columbus was also an
Italian.

Jack That's true.

Rwandan Doctor Perhaps there is a conspiracy.

Jack I'm beginning to think so.

Rwandan Doctor If you will forgive me, I would not stay
long at the *Mille Collines*.

Jack No, we're found a place in Nyamirambo.

Rwandan Doctor I would move quickly from there.

Jack . . . Okay. Is there . . . ?

Rwandan Doctor If I may be candid, your wife should
not be seen at a place like that. To stay there, where
women sell themselves to Western . . . We do not approve
of this. We are not so carefree here. A home is much
better. Some place more private and safe. Safety is very
important here.

*The Doctor rises and a surprised Jack does the same,
as the Orderly steps forward and whisks away Jack's
drink.*

It has been an honour to meet you. I hope your research
is fruitful.

Jack I'm sorry, there's been some sort of – I'm still
waiting to see Doctor Gasana. Your secretary, I told her
this.

Rwandan Doctor Gasana.

Jack Yes. He's the subject of my book. Dr Joseph Gasana.
I'm here to see him.

Rwandan Doctor There is no Gasana here. We have no
one by that name on our staff.

Jack He's the specialist in – He runs your children's HIV
clinic.

Rwandan Doctor Mr Exley, how I dearly wish we had
any specialists on our staff. We have no one by that name
here.

Jack (*pause*) That's not possible.

Rwandan Doctor But it is true.

Jack This is where he works. This is his job.

Rwandan Doctor Someone has led you astray. I'm sorry.
Please give your wife my best.

TEN

Joseph appears again, talking to us.

Joseph Funding has become difficult, of late. We are
stretched far too thin. This is why I am so eager to begin

our work, so that your book will call attention. And what we are doing so dearly needs attention. Ah! Perhaps you will even make me famous! Red carpets and cameras – pop, pop – everywhere I go! You see? You can take the man out of America, Jack, but once he has been you can never take America out of the man.

I have missed you, my friend. There is no one here I can talk to like this. Your presence will be such a help, Jack. I count the days until your arrival.

ELEVEN

The same morning. Linda stands in the living room of a house. A young Rwandan Man who looks to be in his early twenties stands across from her, suitcases at his feet. No one moves. Finally . . .

Linda Thank you for bringing in the bags. That was very kind of you. Merci.

The Man smiles. He crosses to a chair and sits. Linda stares at him. Silence.

Merci beaucoup.

The man smiles, but does not move. More silence.

Au revoir!

Geoffrey enters from inside the house.

Geoffrey I'm going to take the / room in the back, if that's . . .

Linda Do you have any francs for the driver?

Geoffrey (*digging into his pockets*) Uh, yeah, I –

Linda How much should we –

Geoffrey I don't know.

He has money in his hand. He gives a bill to the Man, who rises, takes it and smiles.

Man (*in Kinyarwanda*) Urakoze. [*Thank you.*]

The Man sits back down. Linda and Geoffrey look at each other. Geoffrey hands another bill to the Man, who again rises and takes it with an even bigger smile.

(*In Kinyarwanda.*) Murakoze cyane. [*Thank you very much.*]

The Man sits back down. Silence. Finally . . .

Linda Monsieur –

The phone rings. Linda crosses to it and picks it up. Into the phone:

Allô bonjour? . . . Oh, Mr Mizinga!

The Man stands up.

Yes, we've just arrived. It's perfect. Thank you so much for finding us a . . . Oh . . . That's . . . Yes, we're free today . . . That would be lovely! . . . We'll see you then. And, again, thank you so – (*She listens, then looks at the Man.*) Yes . . . He's right here. (*Pause.*) I see . . . I see . . . (*Pause.*) Of course.

She offers the phone to the Man, who crosses to her and takes it. He listens, then speaks into the phone.

Man (*in Kinyarwanda*) Yego bwana. Narihano ngutegereje nkuko wabyifuje bwana . . . Nibyo bwana . . . Ukubyifuza bwana . . . Ndabyunva. [*Yes, sir. I was right here waiting, as you asked, sir . . . Of course, sir. Whatever you wish, sir . . . I understand.*]

The Man hangs the phone up and starts to exit into the house. At the last moment, he turns back to them.

(*in Kinyarwanda*) Njyewe ndagiye. Mukomere kandi.
[*Welcome, sir. Welcome, madam. I will leave you now.*]

Gérard is gone.

Linda (*to Geoffrey*) . . . His name's Gérard. He works
for us. He lives here.

TWELVE

*That afternoon, the International Red Cross hospital.
Jack is meeting with a male British Doctor. Another
Rwandan Orderly, thin and stooped, stands to the side.*

British Doctor Gasana.

Jack Dr Joseph Gasana. He's / the director of . . .

British Doctor (*remembering*) Yes! The Children's HIV
Clinic at Kigali Central. / Clinical trials with antiretrovirals.

Jack Exactly! Yes. So you know him.

British Doctor Not personally, but I hear he's very good.

Jack But they said he doesn't work there.

British Doctor Welcome to Rwandan bureaucracy,
Professor Exley.

Jack They had no idea who I was even – How do you
know my name?

British Doctor Oh, everyone knows everyone here. Bit
suffocating; wonderful for the gossip. Besides, it's not like
we get a planeload of Americans every day, is it? Well,
now the shooting's stopped, we do get a few. Visit the
gorillas, visit the prostitutes; sort of a package tour. And
by the way, condoms are an absolute must. With the
prostitutes, that is. (*remembering*) But didn't I just hear
that your friend's funding was cut off?

Jack Joseph's?

British Doctor Some sort of trouble with the authorities? (*He turns and speaks in French to the Orderly.*) Connaissez-vous un docteur du nom de Joseph Gasana? [*Do you know a Doctor Joseph Gasana?*] (*to Jack*) You know him well?

Jack Yes. He's one of my oldest friends.

British Doctor C'est un pédiatre. Un specialiste de la prévention du Sida. Il travaille a l'autre hôpital. [*He's a pediatrician. A specialist in HIV prevention, at the other hospital.*]

Orderly Non, je suis désolé docteur, je ne connais pas de Dr Gasana. [*I'm sorry, doctor. I do not know a Dr Gasana.*]

British Doctor Are you sure he's not off at a conference or something?

Jack No! He invited *me*. I got a letter from him just a week ago. He knows his work is the spine of my book. He's in Kigali. He *has* to be here.

British Doctor (*to the Orderly*) Merci, François.

The Orderly nods and slowly shuffles out.

Jack Are you sure he doesn't work here? Could he have transferred or –

British Doctor I'm afraid we don't share staff with their hospital. And if you get sick, with all due respect, make sure you come here.

Jack (*gesturing towards where the Orderly left*) Is he ill?

British Doctor François? He's dying of AIDS.

Jack Jesus.

British Doctor Last of his family. Wife, six children, already gone. You want to talk about stoicism? These people, I'm in awe. Their grace, kindness. To maintain that in the face of AIDS, malaria, sleeping sickness –

Jack You mean like –

British Doctor Something medieval, yes. We've started to get reports from up north. Entire villages, just laying down, falling asleep, and dying.

Jack God, I had no idea.

British Doctor Why would you? You have to be here to start making sense of this place. Before I came I read everything, thought I was a bloody expert. Then I got off the plane. Some things, though, still mystify. Country's organised on a ten-cell model –

Jack Like the Tanzanian system that / Nyerere . . .

British Doctor Precisely. It's divided into ten *préfectures*; tens all the way down to the neighbourhood level. Organisational genius. So why do I see people here every day who are dying because they don't know about medicines that are readily available? What's this vaunted network being saved for? Because if the people running this country ever wanted to do something big, it would happen – (*Snaps his fingers.*) – like that. Perhaps he left, your friend.

Jack Why would he do that?

British Doctor Well he's Tutsi, isn't he? Right now, if I were a Tutsi? Christ, I wouldn't stay here.

THIRTEEN

tands in his light and once again addresses us.

What I see every day, it can be overwhelming. One's faith is tested, Jack. Daily. But what can I do but keep going? Educate the mothers and fathers, see my patients . . . Most of those I see are too young to even know the word. With the limited medicines we have, I save those I can, pray for those I cannot, and think always of Benjamin Franklin. Do you remember that class we took so long ago? I still take my history seriously, Jack. I am *Rwandais* after all. Do you remember what he said? 'The definition of insanity is doing the same thing day after day, but expecting different results.' Benjamin Franklin, *c'est moi.*

FOURTEEN

The same afternoon, Mizinga and Linda inside the Sainte Famille Catholic church.

Linda It's beautiful.

Mizinga Simple, yes. But there is a grace to it.

Linda Really. Just lovely.

Mizinga Sainte Famille is the finest church in Kigali. This is where my family and I worship. Are you Catholic?

Linda Me? No. I'm not much of a –

Mizinga I understand. You are American. Here, we are men and women of God. Catholic, Protestant, even Muslim. A few. For me, this building is our hope.

Linda For what?

Mizinga That God is still watching us. Little Rwanda, clinging to the belly of Uganda. But, still, that we are not forgotten. You do not write things down?

Linda Oh, I don't work like that.

Mizinga Then how are you able to remember?

Linda Well, I'm not a reporter, so I don't . . . It's really not that interesting.

Mizinga But I am interested.

Linda I don't want to take up your time / talking about . . .

Mizinga My time is yours. I insist. Please.

Linda I wait for the ping. (*off his look*) For something that lodges in me that I can't forget. That's my starting point. My husband's work is about the mega; I'm all about the mini. We're always arguing over which is the best way to – Do you follow / what I'm . . . ?

Mizinga (*gesturing for her to continue*) With even more interest.

Linda It has to be a single event. But something complex, with a multitude of meanings, that I can peel back, layer after layer, in order to –

Mizinga Show what is true.

Linda Yes! To bore down to the centre of one incident, until I find it: the bridge that connects something strange and impenetrable to *me*. To the world at large. Showing how connected we are / to each other.

Mizinga We are all the same, then?

Linda Well, I mean . . . on a fundamental level / don't you . . . ?

47

Mizinga You are a bold and forthright seeker of truth!

Linda . . . Okay.

Mizinga I thank you for this. I wish to help you find your moment. To show that here we are men and women, just like you. That this government, we too are dedicated to peace. Of course, there are people here who disagree with that.

Linda You mean, with 'peace' in general?

Mizinga Very many. It is difficult to exist with these people – angry, dangerous – but that is democracy, yes? We are following in the footsteps of our friends in the West. Belgium, France. And of course, the US. We all wish to be friends with the US.

Geoffrey enters.

Geoffrey (*to Linda, speaking loudly and pointing outside*) Did you know that street's named after Kadafi? You know, like, *Kadafi*? I mean / that's kinda –

Linda Geoffrey could you please lower your voice while / we're in the . . .

Geoffrey Don't tell me what to do!

Linda I'm sorry. I was just – / Geoffrey, I'm only saying –

Geoffrey You're not in charge of me! I'm not your little kid! / Dad forget to mention that when he . . .

Linda Well, maybe if you stopped acting like one, I wouldn't feel the need to . . .!

They both stop abruptly. Silence. No one moves. Then . . .

Mizinga (*cheerily*) Did you enjoy your goat?

Lying, simultaneously:

48

Linda / Very interesting.

Geoffrey Definitely. Yeah.

Mizinga Next you must try the fried tilapias. (*picking back up with Linda*) What is heartening is the progress we have made. That we can breathe easier, now that Kigali is finally a weapons-free zone.

Linda And the UN is enforcing this?

Mizinga (*smiles*) May I speak plainly?

Linda Please.

Mizinga The UN . . . It is made up of good people, well-meaning people, but strangers who do not understand what is happening here. You read in your newspapers we are one people, we have had a civil war. But tell me, if the Russians invaded America would you say, oh, this is a civil war? No, because they are foreigners, just like these rebels. Thirty-five years ago they raped and killed us, so we forced them from this land. For thirty-five years they have lived in Uganda. They do not even speak French. These are not *Rwandais*.

Linda You mean the RPF?

Mizinga Of course. And yet, somehow, they are the victims. This is what the UN, their soldiers here, this is what they think. Please tell me, how do foreigners who invade my country, kill my people, and occupy my land, how are these to be victims? Have you perhaps heard your ping yet?

Linda (*smiles*) Maybe.

Geoffrey What were the soldiers singing?

Mizinga Soldiers?

Geoffrey The ones we saw marching in the street.

Mizinga Ah! (*in Kinyarwanda*) Turi guhiga amashu. (*then translating*) 'We are looking' or 'hunting' . . . I am not sure . . . 'for cabbages.'

Linda 'We are hunting for cabbages'?

Mizinga Do your soldiers not chant something like this in America?

Linda Not lately, no.

Mizinga You see, this is the problem. I am translating from Kinyarwanda to French to English. So much is lost.

Geoffrey So if it's weapons-free and all, what's with the tanks?

Mizinga An excellent question. He who wishes for peace prepares for war. For us to rely on the good word of killers, terrorists armed to the teeth, who would do such a thing? (*to Geoffrey*) Would you?

Linda Of course not.

Mizinga We are still shackled to our history here. A spiral of violence. I envy you. In America, you seem to have escaped your history. This is my hope for my country.

Geoffrey . . . Forgetting the past?

Mizinga (*smiles*) To wipe the slate clean and start again.

FIFTEEN

Later that afternoon, Linda alone at a market. She is trying out rudimentary French on a Market Woman selling cabbages. Standing near them is a Market Man.

Linda (*pointing*) Excusez-moi, je voudrais acheter un chou. [*Excuse me, I would like to buy a cabbage from you.*]

The Market Woman smiles, picks up a cabbage, and extends it toward Linda.

C'est combien un chou? [*How much for a cabbage?*]

The Market Woman smiles, nods her head, and extends the cabbage again.

S'il vous plaît . . . [*Please . . .*]

Market Man She does not speak French, miss.

Linda Oh.

Market Man She is from the country.

Linda (*to her*) I'm sorry. (*to him*) Thank you. Could you ask her if –

Market Man Go White Sox! Yes!

Linda Oh. You – yes! The Sox. How do you –

Market Man I was in your country, studying. Many years ago. Chicago.

The Market Woman is watching them intently.

Linda Chicago!

Market Man Yes!

Linda I live in – my family – all of us here – we live in Illinois!

Market Man Illinois!

He turns to the Market Woman and speaks rapidly and excitedly in Kinyarwanda.

Uyu mugore lelo, n'uwo muli Amerika, hamwe nari ndi, muli Illinois! [*This woman is from America, she is from Illinois!*]

The Woman nods and smiles at Linda.

Market Woman Illinois!

Market Man This is what I tell my children.

Market Woman Illinois!

Market Man That this world is wonderfully small.

Market Woman Illinois!

Market Man Eyes open! I tell them.

Market Woman Illinois!

Market Man In this country, if your eyes and heart are open, you will learn many things.

Market Woman Illinois! Yes!

> *The Market Woman gestures to Linda and then to her cabbages.*

Linda I agree. I've found that here. Your country is so fascinating.

Market Man (*translating to the Market Woman*) Avuze ko igihugu cyacu ari kiza. [*She says our country is fascinating.*] (*to Linda*) You are kind.

Linda It's so beautiful here.

Market Man I am grateful to you.

Linda Please. It's an honour to be here. Thank *you*.

Market Woman (*to Linda*) Amashu yange nimabisi cyane. Ngaya, reba, nayasoromye mugitondo. [*My cabbages very fresh. Here, look, I picked them from the earth this morning.*]

Linda (*to Market Man*) Would you mind asking her how much for a cabbage?

Market Man Oh, no miss. (*pointing offstage*) Your shopping should be done there.

The Market Woman is smiling and indicating more intensely now.

Linda Why not from her?

Market Man (*very politely*) She is a filthy Tutsi whore, miss. Her cabbages will be spoiled. She will poison you and you will die.

Silence. The Market Man and Woman look at Linda.

(*pointing*) There, miss.

Linda (*pause, then quietly*) Thank you.

SIXTEEN

Also later that afternoon. Gérard is alone in the living room of the Exley house, reading a book. He holds the text close to his face, reading slowly and out loud. His voice is quiet and we can't make out the words. Geoffrey comes into the room from inside the house. He sees Gérard, who quickly puts the book down.

Gérard Excusez-moi, monsieur Geoffrey. [*Excuse me, Mr Geoffrey.*]

As Gérard starts to exit, Geoffrey sees the book.

Geoffrey Whoa whoa whoa whoa whoa whoa whoa!

Gérard stops.

Tu lisais ce livre? [*You were reading this book?*]

Gérard Oui, monsieur Geoffrey. [*Yes, Mr Geoffrey.*]

Geoffrey Tu sais lire l'anglais? [*You can read English?*]

Gérard Un peu, monsieur Geoffrey. [*I can read some, yes, Mr Geoffrey.*]

53

Geoffrey Est-ce que tu le parles? [*Can you speak English?*]

Gérard Un peu, monsieur Geoffrey. [*Some, yes, Mr Geoffrey.*]

Geoffrey So, you can understand / what I'm saying right now?

Gérard Forgive me. I did not mean to soil your book. I will never touch / it again. Please do not . . .

Geoffrey No, no, no! I didn't mean to – I'm not angry. Really. I'm not. I'm just . . . Why didn't you just, you know . . . tell us?

Gérard A man who tells all is naked. A naked man is weak.

Geoffrey (*considers this*) I'm down with that.

Gérard (*looking down at the floor, then up*) I do not understand / what you are . . .

Geoffrey Yes. I see your point. I respect that.

Gérard I am sorry. My English is very poor. / My school was very short. I was not able, because . . .

Geoffrey No. It's good. It's . . . Sure. I understand. Yeah. You're good. Really.

They stare at each other.

Gérard (*gesturing to the book*) May I respectfully ask what is this book?

Geoffrey American history. Textbook. It's called independent study. So I can graduate.

Gérard You are in school?

Geoffrey Yeah.

Gérard You are a schoolboy?

Geoffrey Well, I'm a senior.

Gérard Here you teach yourself?

Geoffrey Sort of.

Gérard Then you are a smart man. A smart man is a good thing.

Geoffrey My father says that.

Gérard A father knows. Always.

Gérard starts to leave the room.

Geoffrey Listen.

Gérard stops. Geoffrey gestures to the book.

Keep it. Read it. Really. I've got plenty of time. I've got nothing else to do. I'm glad that we . . . I mean, it would be great if we could . . . you know . . . talk.

Gérard (*pause*) You wish to talk to me?

Geoffrey Yeah.

Gérard . . . Now?

Geoffrey Yes!

Gérard I understand.

Silence. No one moves. Then, off Geoffrey's puzzled look . . .

I am respectfully waiting for you to talk to me / Mr Geoffrey.

Geoffrey No! That's not what I meant.

Gérard Forgive me, monsieur / Geoffrey.

Geoffrey Listen. Gérard. You don't have to call me monsieur Geoffrey. Really. I mean it. / Don't . . .

Gérard Of course, sir. / I understand.

Geoffrey No! Not 'monsieur', not 'sir' – My dad is a 'sir'. I'm just – (*Points back and forth between them.*) we're just . . . the same. Right? I'm asking as a favour. I'd appreciate it. Okay?

Gérard studies him.

Gérard You are being honest with me?

Geoffrey Yes. I am.

Gérard (*nods his head and smiles*) I will read this book. I will learn of your country.

Geoffrey Great.

Gérard Perhaps I may show you my country, if you wish.

Geoffrey Yes! That would be awesome!

Gérard Good! / This is good!

Geoffrey I would love that! Totally!

Gérard But if I may ask you a favour, monsieur / Geoffrey . . .

Geoffrey Dude!

Gérard (*smiling*) Sorry! / Sorry!

Geoffrey (*gesturing back and forth between them, exaggerated*) Geoff-rey! . . . Gé-rard! . . . / Geoff-rey!

Gérard (*laughing, doing the same gestures*) Yes! Geoff-rey! Yes! (*then:*) Please tell no one.

Geoffrey . . . What do you mean?

Gérard My English. That I speak. That I know. I ask this as *my* favour.

Geoffrey I'm not really – I mean / what's the big . . .

Gérard The rebels speak English, all of them. If a man like me is speaking English, this man is now a suspect. It is dangerous to be confused with those people. I wish only to go about my business and bother no one. So that I may sleep at night in peace. Please. I ask this of you.

They stare at each other. Neither moves.

Geoffrey.

SEVENTEEN

Late that night, the living room of the Exley house. The sound of a phone ringing. Jack rushes in from another room, followed by Linda, and picks it up.

Jack (*into the phone*) Allô bonsoir? . . . Chuck! Hi. Yeah. I've been out looking for him all day. (*in response*) Everywhere! What have you . . . (*listening, then:*) No, that's – (*Listens again.*) When? . . . How can that . . . (*Listens.*) Okay . . . Okay . . . Thanks. (*He hangs up. To Linda*) Woolsey says Joseph's clinic is closed.

Linda What?

Jack Completely shut down.

Linda When did this happen?

Jack He thinks a week ago.

Linda What for?

Jack He doesn't know.

Linda Does he know where he is?

Jack He says no one does.

Linda Did you know that something like this / might happen?

Jack Of course not! Do you think I would have / brought us here if . . .

Linda So why didn't he –

Jack I don't know!

Jack paces.

Linda I'm sure there's a reason for all of this. Your friend will come by tomorrow, he'll explain everything. (*Pause.*) Jack?

Jack We can't go back, Linda. The house / is rented.

Linda I know.

Jack Joseph is my link. The way in. There's no book without / Joseph.

Linda Jack –

Jack No book means the university is going to let me go!

Linda You'll find him tomorrow. / You'll go to the . . .

Jack THIS ISN'T SWEDEN! (*Pause.*) Sorry.

Linda Listen. We're here. We've got people looking out for us. Mizinga's been very helpful. We're getting settled in. We've got plenty of food. I've even tried goat. (*off his look*) Oh, yeah. Side of the road, grilled, on a stick.

Jack What did it –

Linda Remember that time in Cuzco, when you ordered the cau-cau?

Jack (*screwing up his face*) Oooooh!

Linda And afterward, you had to go to the –

Jack (*shuddering at the memory*) Aaaaaah!

Linda That's what I'm talking about.

They are smiling at each other.

Jack How are you so calm?

Linda I'm from Detroit. You think this is a big deal?

Jack Are you going to write about this?

Linda (*sassy, flirting with him*) Oh, baby. You have no idea.

Jack (*flirting back*) You gonna make me look good?

Linda Well, it all depends on what I get in return.

They kiss.

Jack (*then, quietly*) He's my friend, Linda. What if he's been . . .

Linda Listen. We're going to be okay.

Jack How do you know that?

Linda Because I've got you. Whatever happens here, you've got me, and I've got you. That, I know.

Jack I love you. So much.

They kiss more passionately. We hear a loud car horn outside.

Linda It's Geoffrey. It's just Geoffrey.

Jack What?

Linda He went out. He took the car.

The sound of the front gates being opened.

Jack You let him out alone / this time of night?

Linda He walked out the door before I knew it. / I was calling after him.

Jack You said you would keep an eye on him. / We have to be careful here!

The sound of a car pulling up to the house.

Linda I tried, Jack! I am trying, / every day!

Jack He's just a boy!

Linda He is seventeen years old! What exactly did you expect me to do? Tackle him? / Pin him down?

Jack He's confused, Linda! He doesn't know what he wants! / We have to . . .

Linda You've barely seen him in three years! What do you know about / what he wants?

Jack For God's sake!

The sound of a car door slamming. Their volumes drop instantly.

We're his parents now, Linda! / We can't just . . .

Linda I AM NOT HIS MOTHER! You left her for me! Look at what he has been through! / You want to set the rules, SET THEM!

Jack (*gesturing 'stop talking'*) Shut up!

Geoffrey enters.

(*normal voice*) Hey, sport.

Silence.

Geoffrey Hey.

No one moves. Finally:

Jack So tomorrow, if either of you see Gérard, would you ask him to please tell the guard to stay in front of the house all the time / and not behind the . . .

Geoffrey He doesn't speak English, / Dad.

Jack Right. Sorry. Forgot.

Silence. No one moves.

Do anything interesting?

Geoffrey (*pause*) Yeah.

Silence. Again, no one moves.

Linda I'm going to go in and get ready / for bed.

Geoffrey (*gesturing off*) That guard guy's there every night?

Jack Yes! Just to be safe. Everyone's got one. I mean, it's not just us / because we're . . .

Geoffrey What's his name?

Jack I don't know.

Geoffrey But he's guarding the house, right?

Jack We'll find out tomorrow.

Geoffrey Did you see your friend today, the doctor guy?

Jack We're going to meet soon. There's a lot to discuss.

The phone rings. Linda quickly picks it up.

Linda Allô? . . . (*Pause.*) . . . Allô? . . . (*Pause.*) . . . Bonsoir?

No one is there. She puts the phone down.

Jack Who was it?

Linda gestures that she doesn't know.

(*Pause, then to Geoffrey.*) Everything's fine.

EIGHTEEN

The next afternoon, the living room of the Exley house. Geoffrey is teaching Gérard to sing the hip-hop song 'Whomp! There It Is!'

Gérard 'There's a party over here, a party over there . . .'

Geoffrey 'Wave your hands in the air . . .'

They are both doing so.

Gérard 'Shake the posterior . . .'

Geoffrey (*correcting him, again*) Derrière!

Gérard Derrière! (*back into the song*) 'These three words mean you're getting busy. Who, there she is!'

Geoffrey No, no! 'Whomp! There it is!'

Gérard Ah! (*imitating his hand-gestures and gusto*) 'Whomp! There it is!'

Geoffrey Yeah!

Geoffrey *and* **Gérard** (*together*) 'Whomp! There it is!' 'Whomp! There it is!' 'Whomp! There it is!'

Gérard I prefer Michael Jackson.

Geoffrey No, no, no!

Gérard Michael Jackson is *fantastique*.

Geoffrey Dude, that's so eighties! / That's like death!

Gérard He has the dances, he has the money, he has the Billie Jean. This is my dream. To be in your country, with an American wife, family. Do you miss them?

Geoffrey What?

Gérard Your family in America.

Geoffrey My family's all here. Me and my father.

Gérard And the black wife.

Geoffrey Yeah, and the . . . what you said.

Gérard The white wife, she is in America?

Geoffrey No. She's dead.

Gérard This was your mother?

Geoffrey Yeah.

Gérard I am sorry. This was –

Geoffrey October.

Gérard May I ask how?

Geoffrey We were in the car. After my soccer – football practice. We got hit by a . . . both of us had our seat-belts on. She always . . . I cut my head. That's it. Her head was . . . (*Holds out his hands in front of him.*) Have you ever seen anything like that? When someone's head just . . . (*He closes his hands together.*)

Gérard Yes. (*Pause.*) My family, too. They were killed in October.

Geoffrey . . . Your whole family?

Gérard In Burundi.

Geoffrey That's the country next door, right?

Gérard Here we say, if you wish to know the future, look to Burundi. In October, the Tutsi there, they killed everyone they could. Until the rivers were full of bodies.

Geoffrey They killed . . . the Hutus?

Gérard Yes.

Geoffrey And you're Hutu?

Gérard I am pure Hutu.

Geoffrey Why . . . why did they do that?

Gérard The Tutsi have always killed us. Stolen from us. They are cunning. Even now, they are plotting behind our backs.

Geoffrey But why?

Gérard They are afraid of us. That one day we will stand up and defend ourselves.

Geoffrey Could that happen here?

Gérard In Rwanda?

Geoffrey Yeah.

Gérard That is not a question for me.

NINETEEN

Buisson's office at the French Embassy, the same afternoon. He is being interviewed by Linda. A Servant enters with a tea set on a tray.

Buisson The Khmer Noir we call these rebels. Scorching the earth, emptying the parts of the country they capture of its people. Their general, this Kagame, he is mythic here – larger than life. (*waiving the Servant off*) Bien bien. Ça suffit. [*Good, good. You can go.*]

The Servant leaves the tea and exits as Buisson continues to Linda.

So, what do they call him? The Black *Napoleon*!

Linda Well. Isn't that nice?

Buisson I fear, perhaps, you miss my point.

Linda I fear I do.

Buisson He is not named 'the Black Ike' or 'the Black Schwarzkopf' –

Linda Which sounds like a cocktail.

Buisson Bravo, madame – he is named for a Frenchman. Because Rwanda is part of *la Francophonie*. This is our sphere of influence. Now, of course, *you* wish to have influence here and to supplant us.

Linda Forgive me, but nobody in America even knows where Rwanda is. Do you know how much work it took to find a guidebook in English? Trust me: we don't care / about places we can't find.

Buisson Ah, yes. 'America does not care.' Indochina: you did not care. Kuwait: you did not care. Until, one day, all of a sudden: how deeply you care.

Linda Jean-Claude, again, what I'm interested in –

Buisson If you are so lacking in caring, may I ask why did your government train this Kagame? Why did you teach him how to fight / so that this English-speaking soldier with his English-speaking army could invade an ally of France that has never –

Linda Jean-Claude . . . Jean-Claude . . . (*cutting him off*) *Jean-Claude . . . (She smiles.*) I thank you for meeting with me, and for the lecture, but I'm interested in *you*. Living here, what *you* think.

Buisson Ah, yes. Narratives of self: Nietzsche, Montaigne, Linda.

Linda Time will tell.

Buisson Samuel said you were interesting.

Linda One tries.

Buisson Well. If I am forced to tell the truth, then I would say, living here, I have learned that freedom is vastly overrated.

Linda How pretty that sounds, as you like to say, but would you / be more specific?

Buisson These people – what is the expression? 'Sold a bill of goods'? They have been convinced that above all, one must have freedom. 'Freedom!' with a capital F and an exclamation point and no other thought behind it. That it is better for a people to incompetently, disastrously govern themselves than to be ruled by someone else who was at least passable.

Linda And you were 'passable'?

Buisson Forgive me, but you do not even know the history of this region and you are passing judgement. France was never here. This was a Belgian colony.

Linda So what do you think of them?

Buisson The Belgians?

Linda Yes.

Buisson Do you know how to save a Belgian from drowning?

Linda No.

Buisson Good. We had nothing to do with this nonsense. This *hypothèse Hamitique*. Measuring skulls. Handing out identity cards. You are one race, you are another race. Disastrous.

Linda So as the colonial power, you think the Belgians are responsible / for the problems here?

Buisson Ah, yes! *Le colon*! Everything is always the fault of *le colon*! Please. This is the argument of college students.

This part of the world – Rwanda, Burundi, Zaire – for over thirty years the Belgians have been gone. *We* have been gone. For thirty years these people have made us look like saints. Thirty years they have ruled themselves, and still *we* are to blame? It is very convenient to blame the past. It leaves no time to deal with the present. And this, here, is a present that should be dealt with. How do you find my honesty?

Linda Racist and full of bullshit.

Buisson And I like you, too. I admire your tenacity. Your husband, it appears he is like this as well. Knocking on doors. Asking questions. Tell me, have you found this man?

Linda (*pause*) . . . No. He's still missing.

Buisson How unfortunate. Your husband, he must be very upset.

Linda That's a nice way of putting it.

Buisson May I continue to be honest?

Linda I didn't realise you'd stopped.

Buisson This is not America. Perhaps he would be more effective –

Linda If he kept his mouth shut?

Buisson Please. I am only offering advice, to be discarded if you wish. Discretion. One is more successful here when one is less direct. Here, the straight road is rarely the one to walk.

TWENTY

Joseph speaks out to us.

Joseph If I am honest, Jack, sometimes I wish I were just a doctor. A little practice, treating tourists with dollars and Deutschmarks. That would be nice. I will not lie to you.

But who else is doing what we are doing? We are saving the lives of our children. The future of this country. We are fighting to change this country, Jack. Two steps back, but three steps forward. I would do anything for that. Who would not?

TWENTY-ONE

A bar, that night. Jack sits with Verbeek, thirty, a South African. They have beers in hand, and have already had more than a few.

Verbeek Compared to Sudan or Ethiopia? This used to be the East African success story. Tons of foreign aid, aid workers –

Jack But this was before eighty-nine, right? When the bottom fell out of / the . . .

Verbeek The world coffee market – very good. Now this country doesn't have two nickels to rub together. You throw in over three years of warfare, highest birth rate in Africa, land over-farmed to the point of being useless, and now those motherfucking cocksuckers at the World Bank – you don't work for them, do you?

Jack No.

Verbeek They're threatening to cut off all aid unless Habyarimana implements the BBTG in the next couple of weeks. Well, let's be honest: unless his wife and her cronies tell him to implement. And who came up with this? Because they need more tension here?

Jack But the government's agreed to implement next week, so the peace accords are still / on track.

Verbeek *Agreed* to implement.

Jack Yes, I know, but –

Verbeek You know how many times they've agreed to implement, then come up with a reason not to?

Jack You're focusing on the wrong thing. The point is they've actually achieved multi-party elections here. This country has a chance!

Verbeek Right. And I'm Desmond fucking Tutu.

Jack Come on! You can't be cynical about a democracy when it's just getting started. So they're being dragged to the altar kicking and screaming – fine! It's messy, but it's progress! Democratic elections –

Verbeek STOP TALKING ABOUT THE FUCKING ELECTIONS!

They both look around, to see if anyone's listening. Verbeek leans in closer to Jack and lowers his voice.

Stop thinking like an American. This is Africa, not Delaware but with a lot of black people, all right?

Jack I'm not from Delaware, I'm just –

Verbeek You think you stuff ballots in a box – presto! – problems here get solved? People here are being killed *because* of the fucking elections. The UN forced them down the government's throat, they lost, now they're panicked. Now you've got Hutu elites arming private militias and hoarding weapons. They're not thinking about power-sharing, they're thinking, how many Tutsis do I have to kill to keep what's mine? The engine here's not democracy, my friend, it's violence and fear. Am I making my point, Jim?

Jack Jack.

Verbeek Thanks for the beer.

Jack You're welcome. Thanks for the – (*meaning their conversation*)

Verbeek You're welcome.

They both drink.

Jack So how long have you been here?

Verbeek Just a few months. I need the UN around for my kind of work, so I don't get shot at. Collecting information on human rights abuses doesn't make you particularly popular.

Jack Where were you before this?

Verbeek Mogadishu.

Jack That must have been –

Verbeek Yeah.

Jack So . . . why do you keep doing it?

Verbeek Same reason you're here.

Jack What do you mean?

Verbeek Well, what are *you* running away from?

Jack Nothing. I wanted to come here.

Verbeek Right. Because Paris was full and you thought, 'Hmm, where else do they speak French? Rwanda! That's good.' You alone?

Jack No, I brought my family.

Verbeek You get more interesting by the beer. So what do you teach?

Jack Poli-sci.

Verbeek You got tenure?

Jack You know about the tenure / system?

Verbeek I been around, yeah.

Jack I'm tenure track.

Verbeek Your age, you're still track?

Jack My son was born when I was in grad school, so I took some time off to – it's not that / uncommon.

Verbeek You coming up for review?

Jack After I'm back.

Verbeek First time?

Jack Second, / actually.

Verbeek Aaaah.

Jack That's why I'm here. Research for that book. That I need to finish. Well, start and finish.

Verbeek So you're on sabbatical.

Jack . . . Unpaid leave, / actually.

Verbeek You just get better and better.

Jack There wasn't enough time to submit a proposal. I had to call in favours just to get my courses covered.

Verbeek So it's publish or perish.

Jack Exactly.

Verbeek (*hand to his neck*) Sort of like a blade / to your . . .

Jack Thank you, yes. When you don't get tenured the first time, you beat on doors just to *get* a second position. Some place you used to think you wouldn't even be caught dead teaching at. So you move. You uproot your entire life. And your wife is less than pleased, because the sacrifices to *her* career – and God bless her that she would, but now there's this, this, this *thing* between you, because you've changed the rules, this wasn't the plan. And the clock is ticking, and then – out of the blue! – there's three of you, under the same roof now. So you have to bring him here, too! And you have no idea how to even *talk* to him, because his mother, the wife you fucking left, has been – and the clock is ticking – and you – Aaaaah!

Silence.

Verbeek So everything's riding on this book. About the guy.

Jack Yeah.

Verbeek Who's not here.

Jack He's *here*. He's just –

Verbeek Not here.

Jack (*pause*) Yeah.

TWENTY-TWO

Joseph speaks to us.

Joseph What is hardest, my friend, is the struggle to be patient. In the face of . . . so much. I am *Rwandais*, Jack. No people in the world are as patient as we are. But even I have my limits.

TWENTY-THREE

Late that night, the living room of the Exley house. A ringing phone. Linda enters from another room and quickly picks it up. She does not see Gérard enter as well.

Linda Allô? . . . Allô? . . . Bonsoir?

No one is there. She puts the phone down as . . .

Gérard Excusez-moi, / madame . . .

Linda AH! God . . . I'm sorry, Gérard. I didn't see you there.

Gérard Il y a une jeune femme / qui desire vous voir tout de suite. [*There is a young woman here who says she must see you.*]

Linda Gérard . . . I'm sorry . . . I have told you . . .
Gérard – (*slow and loud*) I DO NOT SPEAK FRENCH!

Gérard (*repeating himself*) Il y a une jeune femme qui désire vous . . .

A Rwandan Woman enters and Gérard stops speaking. He gestures to her.

Là voici. [*Here she is.*]

No one moves as the woman stares at Linda.

Linda . . . Bonsoir.

Woman Good evening.

Linda Oh! Good evening. (*Pause.*) May I help you?

Woman Yes, please.

No one moves.

Linda I'm sorry, I don't think we've –

Woman I am Elise Kayitesi. I am Joseph's wife.

End of Act One.

Act Two

ONE

The living room of the Exley house, later that night. Elise and Jack sit in chairs. Linda stands to Jack's side.

Elise That day, nothing was different. We were to go to dinner after his rounds. I had dressed and was waiting for him.

Linda (*to Jack*) This was last Monday.

Elise Yes, over a week ago. (*to Jack*) He has spoken many times of you. Your friendship. I have sent our children to Butare to be with my family. Joseph is Tutsi, so our two sons are considered Tutsi. It is best they are not here, in case their father has been . . . I do not understand this.

Jack I'm so sorry.

Elise Things have been quiet since he was freed from prison. He has had no troubles with / the government.

Jack Joseph was – what?

Linda Your husband was in prison?

Elise (*pause*) Yes.

Linda When was this?

Elise Three years ago, when the RPF first crossed into the country from Uganda and the fighting began. Men came, Joseph was taken.

Jack Why?

Elise (*pause*) I do not know why he did not tell you this. (*Pause.*) Joseph is a good husband. A good father. / He is . . .

Jack I know that, Elise. Of course. Do you need a place to stay? / You're welcome to.

Elise No, thank you. I must be at home. In case there is any word.

Linda Have you been to the police?

Elise The police are not to be spoken with now. Not for someone like me. Only someone else, someone who is not from here. Only he could find answers.

Pause.

Jack *I'll* go to the police.

Linda Yes. We'll / talk to the police. We'll find out something.

Jack I'll talk to Woolsey again. / Christ, I'll go to UNAMIR!

Elise Thank you! Yes! I thank you so much!

Elise rises to leave.

Linda We'll call you tomorrow.

Jack As soon as I hear anything. I promise.

Elise Please. Even if you know nothing.

No one moves for a moment. Elise turns to leave, then back to them.

My husband is a doctor. He has helped so many people.

She is gone.

Linda How long have they been married?

Jack I didn't even know he was married.

Linda What?

Jack I don't remember him ever . . . it never came up.

Linda Like how being in jail never came up?

Jack Yes. Exactly.

Linda Jack, how long have you known this man?

Jack He's my friend, Linda.

Linda What kind of friend hides things like this? Even from his own wife. What kind of a man is that?

TWO

A police station, the next morning. Jack is in mid-meeting with a Rwandan Policeman.

Policeman Gasana.

Jack That's what I said, officer.

Policeman He has the AIDS sickness, this doctor?

Jack No. No, he wants to stop the spread of – he treats people.

Policeman Tutsi. This doctor works with Tutsi.

Jack Everyone. Anyone / who's suffering.

Policeman Hutu do not get AIDS. AIDS is a Tutsi sickness. Perhaps you did not know this.

Jack Sergeant, my friend is –

Policeman I am a captain.

Jack Sorry, I didn't mean to –

Policeman He is your friend, this Tutsi?

Jack Yes.

Policeman I see. (*Writes something down.*) And you have tried to call him.

Jack Many times.

Policeman You have been to his office / and to his house?

Jack Yes. Yes. Dr Gasana has not been seen in over a week. Something has happened. I am reporting him missing.

Policeman He has gone to Uganda.

Jack What? How / do you . . .

Policeman They all go to Uganda. This is where the *Ibyitso* are. Where they are coming from. All of these Tutsi doctors, they are *Inkoytanyi*. Milk-drinkers. Killers. And now these foreigners, they have made our president, that spineless Habyarimana, grovel and give them our land. They are killing my beautiful, beautiful country. You and your UN and your Bill Clinton, you do not know this. Why does Bill Clinton not know this? We are busy. We do not have the manpower for this. We are preparing to cleanse this country. You are better off without this man. Trust me.

THREE

The Mille Collines, that afternoon. Jack and Woolsey sit poolside.

Woolsey What did you offer him?

Jack What do you mean?

Woolsey The cop, how many francs? (*off his look*) What, they don't have bribes in Sweden?

Jack Damn it! I didn't even think to – / Christ! Like a tourist!

Woolsey It's okay, it's all right. No harm, no foul.

A Waiter has entered with two glasses and two bottles of beer. As Woolsey and Jack speak, the Waiter opens the beers and pours them.

Okay. So you've been to all the hospitals, you've talked to his wife, you've asked around, / no word.

Jack He wrote that he'd be free after the first weekend. That he'd meet me on Monday at the hospital. He was going to arrange for a cook, driver, a translator for my –

Woolsey (*to the Waiter*) Merci.

Waiter (*in Kinyarwanda*) Umunsi umwe uzanywa inzoga nkabagabo. Inzoga Primus! [*One day, you will drink Primus like a real man!*]

Woolsey and the Waiter laugh as the Waiter exits.

Jack (*gesturing toward the Waiter*) What did he just say?

Woolsey No idea.

Jack But you just –

Woolsey Jack, the only Kinyarwanda I know is 'yégo', 'oya', and 'byeri': 'yes', 'no', 'beer'. (*off Jack's look*) Because it doesn't matter. You're working on a book, I'm working on a pension. We're just a presence here. On a map, this country's so small, 'Rwanda' has to be written outside the borders. Little arrow pointing to it, saying 'Actual country, don't forget!' When did you last hear from him?

Jack A week ago. This letter, confirming everything. He was my college roommate.

Woolsey Interesting.

Jack What is?

Woolsey A Tutsi doctor, speaks English, college in the States, not France or Belgium: pretty uncommon. Almost odd, don't you think?

Jack . . . I guess.

Woolsey When's the last time you saw him?

Jack In person? Decade, maybe. We fell out of touch, three years ago. Nothing. Then two months ago, out of the blue, he contacted me.

Woolsey Fell out of touch?

Jack Yeah.

Woolsey Any idea why?

Jack (*pause*) No. He must have just . . . no.

They stare at each other.

Woolsey Jack, things are different here. People, even people we think we know . . . they're not the same here as when they're away from here.

Jack (*pause*) You're saying –

Woolsey You may not have the whole picture.

Jack Meaning?

Woolsey You don't have the whole picture. A lot can happen to someone in ten years, Jack. You need to face facts: he's a prominent Tutsi, doing work that made him stand out. The tall nails are the ones getting hammered here, Jack.

FOUR

*Linda and Elise, at a table inside the Mille Collines, later
that afternoon. A Waiter is opening a bottle of wine and
pouring two glasses as they speak.*

Linda I'm sorry.

Elise Please.

Linda We'll know something about Joseph soon. I'm
sure of it. Jack is – / (*to the Waiter*) Merci.

Elise (*to the Waiter*) Murakoze. [*Thank you.*]

Linda I have a contact at the French Embassy myself. /
I wanted to tell you this in person. And for us to have
a chance to just talk. For you to have a moment, away
from everything.

Elise I am grateful for your help. It has been a blessing.
Thank you. Yes. Of course. Yes.

*The Waiter leaves as Linda picks up her glass of wine,
gesturing to Elise to do the same. She does. Elise holds
back as Linda takes a sip.*

Linda Oh, my God!

Elise Yes.

Linda This is the worst –

Elise Yes. I did not want to be rude. Certain things do
not translate here. (*gesturing to the wine*) This would be
one.

Linda May I ask you a question?

Elise Of course.

Linda What's it like being married to a Tutsi? (*off her
look*) I'm sorry if that's . . . While I'm here, I'm trying

80

to really talk to people. So I can understand this place, and write something that's specific. Honest. For a Hutu like yourself, to have a Tutsi husband, who's been incarcerated – My God, I can only imagine the pressure you're under. I'm asking as a woman married to a man of a different race. Trust me: I know about –

Elise You are blunt.

Linda That's a nice way of putting it.

Elise You are to write about this?

Linda Yes.

Elise All of this?

Linda Yes. (*Pause.*) Elise, / you can trust . . .

Elise leans in and lowers her voice.

Elise Joseph says we are *Banyarwanda*. All of us. Tutsi, Hutu, these are *fabrications politiques*. You understand / what I mean by this?

Linda I do, yes.

Elise The same religion, language. Hutu marrying Tutsi, Tutsi marrying Hutu, Twa marrying / both.

Linda Twa?

Elise Ce sont des pygmées. [*They are pigmies.*] But there are even fewer Twa than Tutsi.

Linda You're saying they're not that many Tutsi?

Elise Here most of us are Hutu. But if you look at us, you cannot even tell from which group we are. Before the Belgians came, Joseph says, Tutsi was just the word for anyone with power; Hutu was the word for anyone without.

Linda But what do you think?

Elise Joseph is much more articulate on this subject. (*She leans in closer, lowering her voice.*) He says that the Tutsi have been made the enemy because it is easier to have an enemy than to find a solution. That since the war started, all of the Tutsi in this country are like hostages. They are seen / as traitors simply for . . .

Linda I want to hear what you think, Elise. Please.

Elise For who?

Linda I'm sorry, / I'm not . . .

Elise For who are you writing? It would be best if I know who I am speaking to before I choose what to say.

Linda Just the truth. As you see it.

Elise (*in Kinyarwanda*) Ukuri kwose sikwiza (*Then translates.*) 'To speak truth is good, but to speak all truth is not.'

Linda I understand, but –

Elise No, you do not. If people like you understood, this country would be very different. We are beaten, we are starved, we are killed, and you do nothing. You do nothing and so it means nothing. To you, we are nothing. (*Pause.*) Now I have become blunt, too.

Linda I'd say so.

Elise It feels quite good.

Linda I can see that.

Elise I will do this again.

Linda I think that's a good idea.

Elise If I am to be killed I wish to save my children. If Joseph is dead, if I am dead . . . (*She hands Linda a piece of paper.*) These are their names. My sons. This is where they are. In Butare. Please do not let them die.

FIVE

Geoffrey and Gérard at a nightclub full of patrons, later that night. They have beers in hand and are yelling over loud, pulsing Zairean pop. A Rwandan Man stands near them, drinking as well. Gérard gestures across the room at a young Rwandan Woman who is dancing.

Gérard You like that one, yes?

Geoffrey Yeah, she's hot!

Gérard Hot?

Geoffrey Totally!

Gérard Hot is good?

Geoffrey *Very* good!

Gérard The Tutsi women, they are all hot. The legs, the breasts. I only sex with Tutsi!

Geoffrey . . . She's Tutsi?

Gérard Look at her, look at me. Can you not see?

Geoffrey *(he cannot)* Okay . . . but . . . your family.

Gérard Yes.

Geoffrey In Burundi.

Gérard Yes.

Geoffrey By Tutsis.

Gérard Yes.

Before Geoffrey can go on, Gérard turns and gestures towards the Woman.

Geoffrey *(grabbing his arm)* Whoa! Don't – What are you doing?

Gérard You do not like her? She must be Hutu?

Geoffrey No! I just – Dude, I don't know enough French!

Gérard Geoffrey, she is not interested in your French. (*as they watch her start to approach*) You must pay her afterwards.

Geoffrey . . . What?

Gérard After you are serviced. If you have dollars, that would be best. (*as they watch her come closer*) Welcome to Rwanda, Geoffrey!

The Woman has danced her way to being in front of Geoffrey. She smiles and reaches out her hand. Geoffrey looks at Gérard then takes it. She leads him out onto the dance floor and they begin to move together. The music heats up. She sways, flirting, touching; he tries to keep up. Gérard watches them. The Rwandan Man does, too. The Woman and Geoffrey yell over the music to hear each other.

Woman Vous dansez bien pour un blanc qui vient d'arriver. [*You dance very well for a white man who has just arrived.*]

Geoffrey Je suis désolé. Je suis americain. Je ne parle pas – [*I'm sorry. I'm American. My French is not very –*]

The Woman throws her head back and laughs, then dances closer to Geoffrey, winding her arms and legs around him.

Woman Tu aimes ça? Et ça, tu aimes? Est-ce que tu me trouves sexy? [*Do you like this? And this? Do you find me sexy?*]

They are pressed together skintight as she bumps and grinds to the music and he tentatively touches her. The Rwandan Man grows agitated by this. Gérard tries to

calm him down. We cannot hear their words. Then,
suddenly, the Man yells at the Woman.

Man (*in Kinyarwanda*) Vana intoki zawe kuri uwo
muzungu, wa ndayawe! [*Get your arms off that white*
man, you whore!]

  The Woman laughs and swivels her hips at the Man.

Woman (*in Kinyarwanda*) Ufite ishyari, wa mbwawe!
[*You're just jealous, you dog!*]

Man (*in Kinyarwanda*) Ziba wa ndaya we y'umututsi!
[*Shut your mouth, you Tutsi bitch!*]

  The Woman and a confused Geoffrey keep dancing.
  The Man lunges, but his way is blocked by Gérard,
  trying to defuse. The Man yells over the music.

/ Nzagaruka, Nzagucamo kabiri! Urunva wa karayawe,
nzagucamo kabiri! [*I'll be back to cut you! I'll cut you in*
two, you hear me, whore? In two!]

Gérard (*in Kinyarwanda*) Ntakibazo, ntakibazo, uyu
musore ni umushyitsi wacu, ntampamvu yo guhangayika.
[*It's okay. It's okay. The boy's a guest in our country. No*
reason to lose your cool. Relax.]

  The Woman laughs again and spits in the Man's
  direction. As Gérard eases the apoplectic Man out of
  the bar, the Man gestures toward the Woman and runs
  his thumb violently across his throat. The music heats
  up. The Woman pushes even closer.

Woman (*in halting English.*) Do you want to sex me?

Geoffrey Yes!

Woman Do you condom?

Geoffrey No, I . . . (*realising*) Yes! Actually, I – I mean,
I wasn't planning, but I –

Woman Will you protect me?

Geoffrey Yes. I mean, sure. (*Pause.*) Yes.

She smiles, takes him by the hand, and starts to lead him upstairs.

SIX

UNAMIR headquarters at Amohoro Stadium, early the next afternoon. Jack stands waiting in a hallway as a Bangladeshi Major brushes past.

Jack Excuse me. Officer! / Excuse me!

Major Sir, you must have an appointment. / I am sorry, but I am too busy to meet with –

Jack I have been waiting outside your office for four fucking hours!

Major Please do not curse, sir. There is no need for cursing. (*Pause.*) I am sorry to hear about this. This is a worrisome thing. My condolences to you, Mr Exley.

Jack Thank you.

Major Now you must go to the police and fill out / the paperwork for . . .

Jack I have been to the police!

Major Then you must go again, that is how things are done in this –

Jack First he doesn't exist. Then he vanishes. Then he's supposed to have gone off to Uganda to, to, to drink milk and start killing people because – I don't know! This man is my friend. Something has happened to my friend. You are the UN, and I am an American citizen! I have come for help! SO HELP ME!

Silence. They stare at each other.

Major Please take off your jacket.

Jack My . . . ?

Major Take . . . off . . . your . . . jacket.

Pause. Then Jack does so.

Lift your arms.

He does.

Turn around.

He does.

Thank you. You may sit.

Jack does so.

One must be careful here about taping and such things. Now, shall we be honest?

Jack Please.

Major Mr Exley, do you speak French?

Jack No.

Major If you will forgive me, that is very foolish. You are seeking answers in a country you do not know, without a language to understand it. And yet you wish me to send my soldiers, who have just arrived from Dakar. You would like us to run through this city, flashing guns, saying, 'A man is missing, and an American wants to know!' 'An American! Oh, my goodness. Shaky, shaky, shaky: here he is.' Mr Exley, we are a small, dirty Band-Aid on a large, festering wound. I am sorry to be so explicit, but I want to be very clear. You promise me you are not taping this?

Jack Yes. I promise.

Major What do you think we can do here?

Jack . . . Help? Protect?

Major Oh, my goodness. We are instruments, Mr Exley. My soldiers, my superiors. For an instrument to be used, there must be a will to do so. For there to be a will, the world must care. This country, these people, do you think the world cares?

Jack I do. Absolutely.

Major I see. The American soldiers, killed last year in Somalia. You know about this?

Jack Of course.

Major Eighteen men, slaughtered. Terrible. But did you know about the ninety UN soldiers killed trying to save those Americans?

Jack . . . No, I didn't.

Major Pakistani and Malaysian soldiers. They were killed and their penises were cut off and put in their mouths. Do you know what a terrible death this is for a Muslim, Mr Exley? Do you not find it interesting that you have not even heard of this? These were not 'marauding savages', terrorist-something-or-others. They were soldiers. Ninety UN soldiers. Unfortunately, with *my* complexion, Mr Exley. If *their* deaths did not matter, what help is there for your friend? He is missing, he has been killed – the world does not care. This is a terrible truth, but it *is* true. A black African man. In this world, what is that? Something not even seen by the eyes of God. I am sorry your friend is Rwandan. I am sorry you are here to know that. I am sorry for this entire, rotten business. Good luck to you.

The Major turns to leave.

Jack Officer.

Major (*turning back*) Yes?

Jack What's your name?

Major How would you know my name? You have never met me.

SEVEN

Linda and Mizinga on the street, the same afternoon, sightseeing Kigali.

Mizinga Do you smell that?

He gestures for her to join him in taking a deep breath. They breathe in and out together.

After it has rained liked this, what do you smell?

Linda It's . . . uh . . .

He gestures for her to take another deep breath; she does so. Exhaling:

Earth, and / a, a, a sort of charcoal, and a, a, a –

Mizinga . . . Yes . . . Good . . . And . . . ?

Linda Eucalyptus!

Mizinga That is it! (*laughing*) You see? You are becoming *Rwandaise*! This is the smell of my country. If I am to show you everything, you must know this, too. I hope you will write all of this. For your people to know my people. I would give my life for this land, Linda. A man must hold his country here, in his heart. He must give his sweat and his blood, so that . . . (*off Linda's look*) Have I said some / thing amusing?

Linda No! What you're saying is moving. I only wish I could . . . It's just, where I live, people like me don't have

89

your level of conviction. Even talk like that makes us /
embarrassed.

Mizinga I understand. The world is different for you. We
are not so lucky. We have a saying here: in Kigali, life
expectancy is twelve hours, renewable.

Linda We have a saying like that back home: (*being
'ghetto'*) yo, watch your back.

Mizinga . . . Yo, wash / your . . . ?

Linda No, no, no. (*hitting the words intently, with full
hand gestures*) Yo! Watch your back!

Mizinga (*imitating her*) 'Yo! Watch your back!' (*Considers
it.*) I like this! I will use this. Now *you* are the teacher.
I thank you / for this.

Linda Thank *you*, Samuel. (*Gestures around her.*) For all
of this. Being here – God! This is exactly what I needed.
I mean, look at me! I look like you. For once, I'm not 'the
other'. My husband, for once, *he's* the . . . Ooooohkay.
Way too much / information.

Mizinga Please. We are friends now, Linda. Friends tell
each other everything.

Linda It's just, all the pressure we've been under, with
Jack having to write this – and now, with Geoffrey! I'm
not equipped for this stepmother business. I'm trying.
I just don't know how to – But being here! It's like a
new beginning. So the three of us – somehow – can . . .

She stares at him. Neither moves. Quietly:

You listen with such intensity, Samuel.

Mizinga (*staring back at her, quiet as well*) We are all
listeners here, Linda.

Linda I'm not used to that.

Mizinga To you? How could a man not listen?

Linda I'm in love with this place, but I'm also scared of it. Can I admit that to you?

Mizinga I believe you just did.

Linda The dichotomy here is . . . vertiginous. Such beauty, such unbelievable . . . but then, things I've heard. Seen. I'm trying to reconcile. I feel a part of this place now, Samuel. I want to understand this place. But I can't / seem to . . .

Mizinga All of life is here, Linda, in one small place. Everything that is said, everything that is done in this world is in Rwanda. That is why life is vivid here. And fearsome. The air is sweet because of this; we are grateful for the time God gives us. You do not understand this place because, where you live, you are too fortunate. You lack an adversary.

Linda You're saying . . . I need an enemy?

Mizinga One is defined by what one is against. And who. To struggle against these people, to fight for what is yours. To suffer and yet to struggle on: this is what makes life precious. And brings understanding. (*He offers her his hand.*) Come. I wish to show you something.

EIGHT

Jack and Verbeek again at the bar, later that afternoon. The men are in mid-conversation, beer glasses in hand.

Jack Who saw this? Who told you this?

A Waiter enters and comes toward them with a fresh bottle of Scotch.

Verbeek Some UNAMIR boys. Wanted to pass on what they'd seen. One of the villages they went through, they found . . .

Verbeek stops as the Waiter arrives and ceremoniously undoes the cap and pours each man a drink, then sets the bottle down between them. Verbeek waits until he leaves, then jumps right back in.

. . . about two dozen people, killed.

Jack Tutsis?

Verbeek That's what they were told. They said the men were cut up with machetes or had their heads cracked open with *masues*, these clubs with nails that – you get the picture. The women had their Achilles tendons cut. So between rapings, they couldn't run. Some of the women who were killed were pregnant. Their stomachs were cut open.

Jack Jesus. Who did it?

Verbeek Don't know. Hutu Power militias, government troops – but something is happening.

Jack Who are you going to tell?

Verbeek I'm telling you, aren't I?

Jack But you have to put this in a report. People have / got to know about this.

Verbeek This isn't enough for a report.

Jack What are you talking about?

Verbeek First rule of reports: you get various sources and you get them confirmed. That's how you find a pattern. That's the only way your narrative makes sense.

Jack But you're not writing a fucking novel. You can't just bury this.

Verbeek You want me to write this without proof?

Jack You can't pretend / you didn't . . .

Verbeek Did I see it? Did you see it? Do you know it happened?

Jack These are UN / observers, for Christ's sake! Why would they lie?

Verbeek Yes, yes, yes. (*off 'lie'*) Because everyone lies here. I'm lying to you right now.

Jack About what?!

Verbeek I'll let you know when I remember. Everyone lies here, Jack. You'll start, too, if you haven't already, Mr I'm-Not-Running-Away-From-Anything. It's self-protection. The question while you're here is: why would this person be honest? Why would they risk that? (*pointing to the bottle in front of them*) You see how they always bring a fresh one, unscrew it in front of you?

Jack Yeah.

Verbeek Now we're supposed to take our first sip together. It's tradition. So we know there's nothing extra in there.

Jack . . . Poison? Are you serious?

Verbeek You mean, am I lying to you? (*He gestures for Jack to drink first.*) Let's find out.

They stare at each other. Jack lifts his glass, and drinks. As he puts it down:

Someone saw your friend.

Jack stares at him.

Jack Who saw him?

Verbeek I asked around and someone said that someone saw him. That's all I'll say.

Jack Recently?

Verbeek Yes.

Jack You mean within the last week?

Verbeek Yes.

Jack Okay. Good. Okay. (*off his look*) What?

Verbeek People didn't want to talk about him. His name made them frightened.

Jack Frightened? He's a doctor! He runs a pediatric AIDS clinic!

Verbeek They linked him to serious business, Jack. Passing on information about weapons caches.

Jack To who? Who is he / suppose to be . . .

Verbeek I'm just telling you what / I heard.

Jack Jesus! The man is missing and no one can give me a straight answer! Woolsey says he's probably dead; you tell me this; Mizinga / tells my wife that . . .

Verbeek *Samuel* Mizinga? You're kidding, right?

Jack No. What's the –

Verbeek Samuel Mizinga is CDR.

Jack I don't know / what that means. I don't speak French.

Verbeek *Coalition pour la Défense de la République.* They're the Hutu extremist party. They wouldn't even sign the Accords. Jack, Samuel Mizinga makes Idi Amin look like a choirboy. He's one of the people calling for the streets to be washed in Tutsi blood.

Jack (*pause*) How do I know this is true?

Verbeek Well now you're getting a handle on things.

Linda on the street with Mizinga, even later that afternoon. They stare out past us at a large building. We hear the sound of soldiers and military equipment.

Linda Are those soldiers actually RPF / guerrillas?

Mizinga Yes.

Linda And . . . they've taken over your parliament / building?

Mizinga The soul of our nation, yes. Like a rebel army, in your White House. Can you imagine? (*pointing*) A battalion of killers, with guns and missiles.

Linda My God, how horrifying. How could this –

Linda has started to move forward, but Mizinga puts his arm out, stopping her.

Mizinga Please. Do not cross this line. Everything on that side has been seized by the RPF. There, you are no longer safe. They are digging tunnels underneath the earth, Linda, preparing for an attack. Reinforcements, ammunition, snuck in every night under / darkness.

Linda Samuel, I / don't . . .

Mizinga It is important you see this. To understand. This is why we are frightened. That what has just happened in Burundi will happen here: Hutu, everywhere, murdered in the streets, the earth soaked in their blood. (*He points again.*) This Tutsi army! They have been attacking us, trying to overthrow, for so long. To push the Hutu back down, so again we are nothing but slaves. These

terrorists, who Habyarimana – that peasant – has allowed
to infect this city, who are protected by your UN, they
are everywhere. Neighbours, so-called friends. Even in
families, loving families, there are Ibyitso. (*Pause.*) Joseph
Gasana.

Linda ... Do you ... How do you –

Mizinga A killer of Hutu children.

Silence. Linda stares at him.

Why do you think his clinic was closed? Giving medicine
only to Tutsi, so that our children would die. You have
been deceived. I am sorry for that. I know this must be
difficult, but you must trust me. You do not know this
country.

TEN

*The police station, that evening. Jack sits before the same
Policeman, who puts on a big show of 'looking' through
the papers in front of him.*

Policeman (*reading from a report*) Gasana, Joseph.

Jack Yes.

The Policeman continues to read.

Captain, you called me. I came out this time of night /
because ...

Policeman Ah, the Tutsi doctor!

Jack Yes! What have you heard about him?

Policeman Yes. We know now, yes.

*They stare at each other as we also see a room above
the nightclub. The Woman who was with Geoffrey the
night before leads him into the room by the hand.*

Jack Where is he?

Policeman Here.

Woman J'ai envi de toi. [*I really like you.*] (*pointing to a chair.*) Assieds-toi. [*Sit down.*]

Geoffrey sits as Jack pulls out his wallet, takes out francs and hands them to the Policeman.
The Policeman counts the francs as the Woman stands behind Geoffrey and begins to massage his shoulders
The Policman starts to exit to the back of the police station. As Jack starts to follow:

Policeman Wait.

The Policeman exits as the Woman pulls Geoffrey's shirt off over his head and drops it on the floor.

Woman T'es vraiment costaud. T'es un vrai mec. [*You are very strong. You are like a real man.*]

The Policeman returns with a gurney with a body on it, covered in a white sheet. The part of the sheet covering the face of the body is red with blood. JACK stares at the body.
The Woman begins to massage Geoffrey's bare chest as the Policeman lifts the cloth. Jack looks down on the figure. The cloth is put back down.

Woman Tu veux essayer autre chose? [*Would you like to try something different?*]

Geoffrey nods and the Woman crosses and kneels down in front of him, her back to us. She undoes his pants and begins servicing Geoffrey.

Policeman His identity card was in his trouser. Down around his ankles. He was found on the side of the road, where these men go to see their Tutsi whores.

The Policeman wheels the body off as the Woman stops for a moment.

Woman Est-ceque tu aimes ça? [*Do you like this?*]

Geoffrey nods and she goes to back to it as the Policeman returns.

Policeman What can we do? These cockroaches: they breed with each other, then kill each other. It is their blood, this sickness.

The Woman continues and Geoffrey is breathing heavily.

Jack I want an investigation into his murder.

Policeman Sir, I am telling you. There is nothing to be done.

Jack I will go to my embassy, do you understand? Do you understand?

The Woman is moving faster now. Geoffrey's breath is hard, sharp.

Policeman Kigali is a very dangerous city. I am sorry to be the one to tell you this, Mr Jack William Exley living in Nyamirambo, on sector Nyakabanda, in the house with the blue door. Terrible things can happen here.

Geoffrey spasms, throws his head back and gasps.

ELEVEN

Late that night at Woolsey's front door. Woolsey stands inside the doorway. Jack stands outside.

Woolsey Who else have you / talked to about this?

Jack No one. I came here, from seeing the . . . Jesus.

Woolsey I'm sorry, Jack. Truly sorry.

So. Your book. What are you gonna do?

Jack FUCK MY BOOK! The man is dead. His face wasn't even . . .

Silence.

Woolsey You go home. Tell Linda and your boy to stay put. I'll speak to UNAMIR, see if they can spare a couple of men, just to check in with you the next few nights. Everything's going to be fine.

Jack 'Fine'?

Woolsey For your family. Look, I understand / that this has been a hell of . . .

Jack I want this investigated. I want to find who –

Woolsey We're not going to do that. (*The two men stare at each other.*) This isn't our country. We don't make the rules here. You're going to have to let this go. A man was in the wrong place at the wrong time. Tragic. Truly.

TWELVE

The living room of the Exley house, very late the same night. In the dark, we can make out the form of a man, sitting in a chair. After a moment, Jack enters from outside. He closes the front door. As he starts to cross the room . . .

Man Hello, / Jack.

Jack Jesus!

Man I hope you are well.

The men stare at each other. Neither moves.

Jack Hello, Joseph.

Joseph You look like you have seen a ghost. I am not a ghost.

Jack starts to move to a lamp to turn it on.

Please.

A moment, then Jack takes his hand off the lamp.

Jack I thought you were dead.

Joseph Yes.

Jack You're not dead.

Joseph Forgive me, but you say this like this is not a good thing.

Jack How long have you . . . Did you plan this?

Joseph Jack. This is me. Joseph.

Jack Where have you *been*? Why didn't you –

Joseph It is only me. I am nothing but me. I have tried to call you. Many times. But it was never you who answered. I have been waiting for a moment to see you. When it was safe for me.

Jack Now that you're 'dead'.

Joseph Yes.

Jack Who was that I saw?

Joseph I do not know. I have prayed for him.

Jack So you faked . . . What is this?

Joseph I am just trying to stay alive.

Jack Because people –

Joseph Yes.

Jack Why?

Joseph I have lists. Of names. People who are to be killed. Hundreds of people. Help me, Jack. Please.

They stare at each other.

Jack Do you know these people?

Joseph Of course. Everyone knows everyone in this city.

Jack So who are they?

Joseph They are like me: doctors, lawyers, teachers. Some are Hutu, some are Tutsi.

Jack So none of them are affiliated with –

Joseph Yes, some are politicians. / But they are moderates, they are the people who are trying to . . .

Jack I mean, are any of them involved in any kind of secret –

Joseph 'Secret'? Yes, Jack. We are all secret agents. My code name is Chuck Norris.

Jack So what have they done?

Joseph Nothing. That is the problem. We are in a civil war, Jack. To not choose a side, this is as bad as choosing the wrong one.

Jack So who's behind these lists? The government? The Interahamwe? CDR's militia?

Joseph Very good, my friend. For me they are all the same. They are all Hutu Power: extremists and extremist-extremists. They are arms of the same octopus.

Jack So who am I supposed to trust?

Joseph Besides me, you mean? You are like me, Jack. We are outsiders. Teacher, doctor. You are not French, Belgian, NGO. You have no history here. That is a gift. A weapon.

Jack Joseph. What am I supposed / to do?

Joseph You are American, Jack! You will be listened to!

Jack For God's sake! I'm / just a . . .!

Joseph You can get these lists into the hands of people who will protect. You can get my family and me out of this country. (*Pause.*) Only you.

Jack starts to pace, back and forth.

Jack Okay, okay, so I'll go to the UN. I've / been there, already met a –

Joseph No, they are useless. Paper soldiers.

Jack UNAMIR's got two thousand armed –

Joseph MINUAR, Jack. The French acronym is MINUAR.

Jack They've / got soldiers who can –

Joseph In Kinyarwanda it means, 'Your lips are moving but you are saying nothing.' It is good to know that someone in the UN has a sense of humour.

Jack Then I'll go straight to the French Embassy and / meet with . . .

Joseph Jack! Please! Open your eyes! You have not been paying attention!

Jack They're the only ones with connections! There are fifteen US officials in this entire city! The French can / find out whoever's behind this!

Joseph Their soldiers fought the RPF! There is only still a war because of the French! Their hands are soaked in the blood of my countrymen! Mitterrand's own son is selling the weapons that are killing our women / and children!

Jack WELL WHAT THE FUCK, JOSEPH! WHAT THE FUCK!

The two men check that no one has been woken by Jack's outburst. Silence. They look at each other

Joseph It is so good to see you. (*Pause.*) I am sorry, my friend. There was no one here I could turn to. Who else could I / trust with . . .

Jack My son is here, Joseph. My wife and / my son.

Joseph I told you to come alone, Jack. If I had known, I would never have –

The sound of a car honking and the front gates being opened. Both men leap to their feet.

Jack It's okay, it's okay! Joseph! It's just Geoffrey. / He goes out and –

Joseph Jack, no one can know I'm alive.

Jack Of course. / I won't . . .

Joseph Not even Linda.

Jack Joseph, I have to. She's my wife!

Joseph She has been talking to the people trying to kill me, Jack.

Jack What?

Joseph They know everything she says and does. Trust me!

Before Joseph can exit, Geoffrey enters from outside and stops when he sees the two men. No one moves.

Geoffrey (*to Joseph, in Kinyarwanda*) Mwiriwe. [*Good evening.*]

Joseph Good evening.

Geoffrey Oh. Cool.

No one moves.

Jack Geoffrey, / this is –

Joseph (*to Geoffrey, in Spanish*) ¿Puede ser que hablas español, joven? [*Do you speak Spanish, perhaps, young man?*]

Geoffrey Uh . . . (*in Spanish*) Un poco. Si. ¿Como lo sabes? [*Some. Yes. How did you guess that?*]

Joseph points at Geoffrey's Che Guevara T-shirt.

Joseph Tu camiseta. ¿Admiras al Che? [*Your shirt. Do you admire Che Guevara?*]

Geoffrey Fue un regalo. De esta chica. [*It was a present. This girl.*]

Joseph ¡Ah! Un regalo de una chica. ¿Era bonita? [*Ah! A present from a girl. Was she pretty?*]

Geoffrey Sí, era bonita. [*Yeah, she was pretty.*]

Joseph Un regalo de una chica bonita. Eres dos veces bendecido. [*A present from a pretty girl. You are twice blessed.*]

Geoffrey ¿Usted es el medico? [*You're the doctor?*]

Joseph I am one, yes.

Geoffrey That Dad's writing his book on?

Joseph (*pause*) I am he.

Geoffrey How's it going?

Joseph Splendidly.

No one moves. Finally . . .

Joseph I must be going. (*to Geoffrey*) It was very nice / to meet you.

Jack Go in the back, Joseph.

Joseph and Jack stare at each other.

Joseph (*to Jack*) Thank you, my friend. (*He turns and looks at Geoffrey. Pause. Then in Spanish*:) Un placer. [*A pleasure.*]

Joseph exits into the house. Neither Jack nor Geoffrey move. Finally . . .

Jack Geoffrey. I need to / ask you –

Geoffrey What's going on?

Jack Everything's fine. I promise. (*Pause.*) I don't want you to tell anyone you've seen that man.

Geoffrey . . . Not even Linda?

Jack No one. I need you to trust me. I need to be your father right now. Please give me your word.

Neither of them move.

Geoffrey Okay.

THIRTEEN

Geoffrey and Gérard in the car, the next morning. Geoffrey is driving.

Gérard Slowly! Slowly! / These dirt roads, you will crack the chassis! You should not go driving when you are angry, Geoffrey!

Geoffrey Sorry. Forgot. Sorry. Look, I'll be more careful!

Gérard A woman should not speak to you like that.

Geoffrey Don't worry about it.

Gérard Stand in your way, try to block you from going out. Jumping about like some chicken.

Geoffrey I said it's cool!

Gérard Cool?

Geoffrey Yeah.

Gérard Cool . . . ?

Geoffrey Means good.

Gérard Like hot?

Geoffrey Exactly.

Gérard Cool is good *and* hot is good?

Geoffrey Yes.

Gérard *Fantastique!* When I go to America I will say – (*pointing*) 'This is cool,' and 'That is hot,' and I will sex all the women. (*off Geoffrey's laugh*) Why not?

Geoffrey All of them?

Gérard Yes!

Geoffrey Dude, we got a lot of women!

Gérard You watch me, Geoffrey! I will sex the black woman, the white woman, the thin woman, the fat woman – Mmmm! The fat American woman! (*making thrusting sounds and hip movements*) Mmmm! Mmmm! (*off Geoffrey's laughter*) Ah, ah, ah! This is your problem!

Geoffrey What? / What are you talking about?

Gérard You are embarrassed. Look at you: you are a pink man now! I see you. I watch you. You talk about a woman like you talk about a man. *Treat* a woman like a man. Like there is no difference. Did God not make us different? You give away your power, Geoffrey!

Geoffrey Dude, I'm not / giving away anything.

Gérard Then why did you let the black wife speak to you like that?

Geoffrey Look, she's my / dad's wife.

Gérard You should not let the black wife –

Geoffrey Linda. Her name's Linda. And don't – she's not black. She's African-American.

Gérard . . . I do not understand.

Gérard We don't say black any more. We say African-American.

Gérard She is from Africa?

Geoffrey No. Her people – you know, at one time, her ancestors were – it's just what we say. To be respectful.

Gérard Of who?

Geoffrey Of . . . the people . . . who . . . I don't know!

Gérard But she is American.

Geoffrey Yes!

Gérard She is not African, she is American. *You* are American, *I* am African. How can one be African *and* American? If you are American, you are American. Who does not know this?

Geoffrey Yeah, but she's an American *and* she's – Okay. In America, okay, the white people, you know, like me, we have the power. We control . . . pretty much everything. So –

Gérard Ah! You are Tutsi! The white man is the Tutsi! / (*joking*) I am in the car with a Tutsi!

Geoffrey No, man! That's not what I'm –

Gérard (*putting his head out the window, pretending to cry for help*) Aaaaaah! Tutsi! Aaaaaah! (*back to Geoffrey*) You are like the man hiding in your house.

Geoffrey stares straight ahead.

Geoffrey What are you talking about?

Gérard The Tutsi your father is hiding. Who is he hiding from? Why would he need to be hiding?

Geoffrey . . . How did you know he's –

Gérard I am frightened, Geoffrey, to be in your house with this man. I am too frightened to sleep in your house. Here, no one is sleeping in their houses. In our village at night, my wife is taking our children to the church.

Geoffrey You have a . . . what? Why / aren't they – I don't . . .

Gérard Home is not safe. Everyone is waiting.

Geoffrey For what?

Gérard I pray to know. But God does not tell me. You are my friend.

Geoffrey I know.

Gérard I am your friend.

Geoffrey Yeah. Totally. (*Looks at him.*) Yes! Of course.

Gérard Then I am asking you.

Geoffrey (*pause*) What do you mean?

Gérard To go. To leave with you. I will get my family, and we will –

Geoffrey Gérard, I'm not – we're not going anywhere. / We just got here. My dad's book isn't even . . .

Gérard You will leave soon, Geoffrey. Do you think this is a place for you to stay? (*cutting him off*) *Something is coming.* Closer, closer. I do not wish to be here to see it. I will do what I must. But to go, I would only need –

Geoffrey You want me to, to take you to –

Gérard Please.

Geoffrey I'm just . . . what can I do? I'm just a . . . I mean . . . What can I do?

They drive in silence as they stare straight ahead.

Gérard I understand.

FOURTEEN

The driving range at the Kigali Country Club, later the same morning. Woolsey is dressed to play, club in hand. Jack has just arrived, out of breath.

Woolsey Jack! What are you stalking me now?

Jack I called your office. / They said . . .

Woolsey (*crouching, getting ready to hit a ball*) Christ, I wish you played. I always get teamed up with some Belgian. Ever played competitive sports with a Belgian? There's a reason the whole empire thing never worked for those people. And the French! The way they treat the caddies is . . .

He unwinds and hits his ball. The two men watch the long, arcing shot go on and on. Then Woolsey drops another ball and continues on.

. . . unbelievable. Like they think they're still running this part of the world. That little Parisian snot Jean-Claude, out here, last week –

Jack I have some information.

Woolsey Since last night?

Jack Yes.

Woolsey Something you want / to tell me?

Jack Yes.

Woolsey Good. Okay. (*Pause.*) Is this a twenty-questions thing? Because / I can –

Jack People are going to be killed.

Pause. Woolsey gestures with his hand for more.

There are lists.

Woolsey . . . Of people?

Jack I've seen them, yes, hundreds of people. These are Hutus and Tutsis. All walks of life. They're not involved in – Regular people. Something is going to happen.

Woolsey I know.

They stare at each other.

Jack / You –

Woolsey I live here, Jack.

Jack So . . . ?

Woolsey What?

Jack . . . *Stop this.*

Woolsey Jack, I've told you. We are strangers here. There are two-hundred-fifty Americans here. This whole country, that's it. / There are two-hundred-fifty million of us back home. Whatever is going to happen here, how important do you think –

Jack I am coming to you. I am a citizen. I am reporting a crime to you. Men and women are going to be killed.

I am a citizen, and – (*cutting him off*) YOU ARE MY
FUCKING GOVERNMENT.

Woolsey gestures to him: 'Lower your voice!'

So help me, I will find a way to –

Woolsey Go over my head? Call in the marines? Okay.

*Woolsey goes back to his game and drops another ball.
He rears back, club over his shoulder, ready to hit –
then turns to Jack.*

You gonna send your son with them?

Jack What?

Woolsey These lists. What would *you* give up to save
these people, Jack? Would you send Geoffrey?

Jack That is not –

Woolsey Ho, ho, bullshit, yes, it is. Boots on the ground,
mission of mercy, we sweep in – who's the 'we', Jack?
Some trying-to-make-it-to-college kid from the Bronx?
Some eighteen-year-old cow-tipper from Illinois? They
should come here? Risk their lives to save some people on
some list because it's the right thing to do? You teach
poli-sci, Jack. When in the history of the world has there
been a country with a foreign policy based on 'it's the
right thing to do'? People are killed. Every day. All over
the world. That *is* the world, Jack. Would that it were
not. Who gave you these lists?

They stare at each other.

Jack I don't know them.

Woolsey Someone who knew your doctor? The one
who's supposed to be dead?

Jack I never saw them again.

Neither man moves.

Woolsey When you find yourself in a hole, Jack, stop digging. I made some phone calls this morning. I have some things to tell you about your doctor friend. You're gonna want to hear them. Trust me.

FIFTEEN

The Exley home. Same day, same time. Linda and Elise, who is shaking. Gérard stands to one side.

Elise Again, I am so sorry / to bother you. But this is where I had to come.

Linda Please. Please. It's fine. I just wish I knew where Jack was. I got up this morning, he was already off doing – God knows what.

Elise The men, I don't know how they entered. I woke up and they were –

Linda Did they hurt you? Did they –

Elise (*shakes her head vigorously*) No.

Linda Was anything stolen?

Elise They were not there for that. They were searching. Under the bed, the bathroom, the kitchen storeroom. One of the men had a gun. He put it in my face. 'Your husband is a traitor. When I find him, he will die slowly.'

Linda (*dismissing him*) Merci, Gérard.

Gérard nods and exits.

Elise I must go to Butare. From there I will try to get our children to Burundi. Please tell Joseph this. Tell him they know and they are coming for him.

Linda (*pause*) Elise . . . Last night, Jack got a call from the police. He had to identify a body. It was Joseph's.

They stare at each other.

Elise This is not true.

Linda I'm so sorry. I know this / must be . . .

Elise That body was not Joseph's.

Linda . . . How do you . . . ?

Elise Your husband told me this.

Linda stares at her.

He phoned me late last night, to tell me Joseph was alive and somewhere safe. He warned me of the lists and promised me he would give them to the people who will protect us.

Linda What lists?

Elise Those who are marked to die. Why has your husband not told you all this?

They stare at each other.

Please, tell him to tell Joseph where I am going.

She starts to leave, then turns back.

Do not trust a husband who does not trust you.

SIXTEEN

Sound of a thunderclap, a downpour. The living room of the Exley home, late that afternoon, dark from the storm. Geoffrey is crossing to the front door – then stops. He realises someone else is the room.

Geoffrey (*in Kinyarwanda*) Ninde uri munzu? [*Who's there?*]

Geoffrey turns on a light. They stare at each other.

Joseph You have Carol's facility with language.

Geoffrey (*pause*) When did you meet –

Joseph When you were a child. I held you in my hand. Your mother put you in this one hand. You were delicate and so very small. I am sorry, Geoffrey. I liked her very much. (*gesturing to the front door*) Where are you going?

Geoffrey Out.

Joseph With your father and Linda not here? Do they know / you are . . .

Geoffrey Just going to see someone.

Joseph The same 'someone' you were seeing last night?

Geoffrey Why is everyone here killing each other?

Joseph Rats and cats, cats and rats.

Geoffrey That one doesn't really translate.

Joseph For the rat, there is no animal more dangerous than the cat. It is all he sees, all he thinks of. Because the cat, he spends each day trying to kill the rat. For if he does not, and the rats become more and more, who will be the hunter then? It is not hatred that drives them both, it is fear. We are trapped in a cycle. Prisoners, of each other.

Geoffrey Have you killed people?

Joseph Of course not. I am a doctor. I am a man like your father.

Geoffrey I don't know my father.

Joseph He is your father. What else do you need to know? Who has been here?

Geoffrey You mean / visiting my –

Joseph Yes. To see Linda, your father.

Geoffrey Or me? Like who's been visiting me?

Joseph Have you had visitors?

Geoffrey Is there a reason I should tell you that?

Joseph (*gesturing offstage*) The one waiting for you in that car, who is *that* man?

Geoffrey Gérard works here.

Joseph And you trust him?

Geoffrey Yeah.

Joseph You are fortunate.

Geoffrey He's my friend.

Joseph Then you are twice blessed.

Geoffrey What are you doing here?

Joseph I am staying here.

Geoffrey Why?

Joseph Some things one should not ask. Trust is to be earned. Is it not?

SEVENTEEN

Buisson's office, the French Embassy, late the same afternoon. The sound of rain. Buisson and Linda are in mid-conversation.

Buisson (*reading from notes*) Kayitesi.

Linda Elise Kayitesi. I want to know if there's a way she and her children / can be protected.

Buisson May I ask what you know of this woman?

Linda She's a Hutu. She's, she's just a mother. Elise isn't affiliated with any sort of – She's not involved in anything.

Buisson And where is she in Butare?

They stare at each other.

Linda, I cannot help if you have no information.

Linda This is her address.

Linda hands him Elise's piece of paper.

Buisson And the husband?

Linda He's dead.

Buisson What did he do?

Linda I don't know anything about him. Just that he's dead.

Buisson Who have you spoken to about this?

Linda I'm speaking to you.

Pause. Buisson puts the papers down.

Buisson I will make phone calls. / I will inquire and see what can be done . . .

Linda Thank you. Thank you so much.

Buisson . . . if you are honest with me. (*Pause.*) This was the doctor. This 'dead' husband. Yes? The one *your* husband –

Linda I've never met him. Please believe me. I don't know / anything about this man.

Buisson 'Man is evil, but woman is base.'

Linda . . . Excuse me?

Buisson Our friend, Friedrich / Nietzsche.

Linda Yes. Right.

Buisson I do not agree, of course, but I admire his honesty. And now I am going to continue down *our* path of honesty. These people here kill each other, Linda. Violence is always beneath the surface. Like a watch, ticking. Those in power kill those out of power with an almost biological regularity. They are tribal. It is in the blood. This is shocking and brutish, yes, but it is also true. It is my job to protect people like you and help those on our side.

Linda 'Our side'?

Buisson Do not confuse diplomacy with missionary work, Linda. In this world, sides are always chosen.

Linda She's a woman with two children.

Buisson Whose husband you know nothing about. You have no context, Linda, and, as we discussed, that is a dangerous thing. Joseph Gasana is a spy for the RPF. He is a terrorist, with blood on his hands.

He takes out a folder from his desk.

Things that have not been seen, they are hard to imagine. I think you should see these things. Perhaps then you will wish to tell me everything you know, to help us find this man.

He slides the folder across to her.

Understand, Linda: you are now involved with serious business. As serious as it gets.

EIGHTEEN

*That night, Geoffrey and the Woman in the room above
the nightclub. The sound of rain mixes with throbbing
music from downstairs. They have had sex and are
getting dressed. Geoffrey has been drinking.*

Geoffrey My dad took me. Him and my mom. When I
was a kid. This island. (*gesturing off into the horizon*)
Waaaaaaay out. These beaches and it was so *still*, you
know? Can't forget something like that. The, the, the
clarity! Can you understand / what I'm saying?

Woman I sex good?

Geoffrey Yeah, Emiritha, I've got more francs.

*He takes out his wallet and gives her money. He stares
at her.*

I thought this was gonna . . . (*Gestures between them.*)
This was gonna be about you and . . . it's not like that.
You know? It's / all just . . .

Woman You will protect me? / Please?

Geoffrey Yeah. Of course. Just let me finish my –

Woman Je viens avec? [*You take me?*] You take me? Yes?
Please? Geoffrey? / You . . .

Geoffrey Listen! Okay? I'm just . . . I'm just trying to –
what are *we*, people like *me*, supposed to – You know
what I mean? This fucking country is just . . . sorry . . .
I don't understand why everyone here is . . .

*The Woman kneels in front of Geoffrey and begins to
undo his pants.*

I don't want to be here.
   I don't understand this place.
   I hate this fucking place.

Geoffrey pushes her hands away and exits, leaving her in the room.

NINETEEN

Jack and Verbeek, the same night, moments later. They are again at the bar, mid-scene. We hear the rain coming down fiercely outside.

Jack Joseph Gasana. What *exactly* have you heard?

Verbeek I told you what I could. People said he was mixed up with dangerous things.

Jack I've just been told things things about Joseph. Specific things I need to corroborate / to know if they're true.

Verbeek Look! I'm sorry that your friend is dead, but –

Jack He's not.

Verbeek . . . Okay.

Jack So, please: *who* told you, and what *exactly* / did they . . .

Verbeek Jack! Maybe your friend's who you think he is, maybe not. Maybe he's done things, maybe not. You want to be certain? You let him take the first drink.

As Verbeek starts to leave, Jack grabs his arm.

Jack I need your help. I have lists of people. / I have no one else I can – listen to me! – names of people in this city who are going to be killed!

Verbeek (*trying not to be overheard*) No. I can't do that. That would compromise my position. I don't – Stop telling me. Stop – (*off 'names', silencing him*) Shut up shut up SHUT UP. You want to get involved, that's your choice. You think you can make a difference, go ahead. I . . . don't . . . get . . . involved. Because I have seen what happens.

TWENTY

The room above the nightclub, moments later. The Woman is waiting for Geoffrey to come back. Gérard and the Man from the club enter the room. The Man has a machete. Gérard covers the Woman's mouth and helps the Man drag her out of the room, downstairs, and through the empty nightclub. Gérard watches from the doorway as the Man takes the Woman out of the front door and offstage.

Gérard watches the Woman be killed. He turns back into the nightclub.

Gérard Geoffrey! . . . (*Silence.*) . . . GEOFFREY!

Geoffrey enters from upstairs.

Geoffrey Hey! Where's the music?

Gérard I should not have brought you here. I am sorry.

Geoffrey Where is everybody? / What happened to all the . . . ? (*He mimes people dancing.*)

Gérard Geoffrey, we must go now.

Geoffrey (*pointing towards the front door*) Where's Emiritha? / Is she already . . . ?

Gérard She is gone. (*pointing toward the back door*) We go this way now.

Geoffrey goes towards the front door.

Geoffrey No, I didn't pay her enough. Can't be rude like that.

Gérard puts himself in his way, trying to stop him.

Gave her the wrong colour bill – (*shoving Gérard*) GET THE FUCK OFF ME!

Gérard Come – Geoffrey – Geoffrey –

Geoffrey pushes past him and goes to the front door. He sees the Woman's body.
Neither man moves. Geoffrey puts his hands over his mouth.

Geoffrey She . . . She's . . .

Gérard crosses to Geoffrey. They both look out of the front door.

Gérard God is not watching us now, Geoffrey. We are alone. We all must do what we must do.

TWENTY-ONE

The living room of the house, very late that night. Jack and Linda are mid-argument.

Jack You did what?

Linda Jack, I gave her my word! / I can't just sit here and do nothing while everything is –

Jack Mother of God, Linda! What were you thinking?

Linda What? Exactly what, Jack? What did I do wrong?

Jack The French are not to be trusted. / Not here. We can't . . .

Linda 'The French'? You're making statements like 'The French' now? This is all the rage in Political Science? 'The French', / 'the Africans', where else can we go with this?

Jack We have to, we have to be careful! This isn't –

Linda Detroit? Thank you. I was so confused about that.

Jack You know what I mean!

Linda I don't know one damn thing.

Neither moves.

Where is he?

They stare at each other.

Jack I don't know.

Linda Don't. Don't. Where is he?

Joseph enters from the door leading to the bedrooms.

Joseph Good evening. (*Pause.*) I am Jospeh. You must be Linda. It is an honour to meet you.

Linda stares at him.

Linda (*to Jack*) How long has he been here? How long have you known / he was still alive?

Jack Linda, people are looking for him. What did you want me to do?

Linda 'What did I want / you to . . . '?

Joseph Linda, you cannot trust the CDR. Samuel Mizinga is a killer.

Linda (*to Joseph*) Are you part of the RPF?

Joseph I am a doctor. I work with children / who are sick from HIV.

Linda Children? You work with children? (*to Jack*) He let Hutu babies die, Jack. So he could save all the medicine for the Tutsi / children in his clinic.

Joseph That is a lie! You think we have medicine for everyone? Have you learned nothing here? I could only give treatment to those who had a chance to live! I am to save half from one group, half from another? My patients are not Hutu, they are not Tutsi, they are children!

Jack Joseph. Answer the question.

Joseph Do not forget who we are, Jack. It is me, Joseph. It is only me!

Jack Are you involved / with the RPF?

Joseph Are my hands clean? Is this what you want to know? Am I spotless? Is that what you need me to be? Hands as white as yours?

Linda (*to Joseph*) I have been shown photos of bodies. People killed by the RPF. / People *you* helped to have murdered!

Joseph Those were government soldiers killed! Not women, not children – but rapists and killers!

Jack Jesus, / Joseph!

Joseph I gave information! That is all! The RPF is trying to save this country, Jack. Not Hutu, not Tutsi, but all of us! We have no choice but to fight until –

Linda It's 'we' now? / Now it's turned into 'we'?

Jack How could you lie to me like –

Joseph OPEN YOUR EYES. WHERE DO YOU THINK YOU ARE?
 (*To Linda.*) The people who have whispered in your ear, who you tell things to – Your friends, who rape a woman and cut a woman. Do you know what they will do if they find my children?
 (*To Jack.*) You think I stopped writing because I was too busy? The RPF entered the north to liberate and I was jailed for being a doctor and a Tutsi. In a hole, chained like an animal. Beaten for sport.

Jack Why didn't you tell me?

Joseph They let me out, you think I am free? Letters are read. People are watched. I wrote everything to you – *between* the lines. How could you not see?

Linda (*to Jack*) I don't trust a word out of his –

The sound of a gunshot in the distance. Blackness as the lights cut out.

Jack Jesus Christ. What was, / what was – what is that?

Joseph The generator. Jack, go! Turn on the generator.

Another gunshot. The sound of a car pulling up and honking over and over.

Joseph / Quickly! You must!

Linda Is that Geoffrey? Jack! Is that Geoffrey?

Jack (*to Linda*) I don't know!

Sound of a car door slamming.
Sound of gunfire. Closer.

Geoffrey (*offstage, calling from outside*) Dad! . . . / Dad! . . . Dad! There are people outside! Lights are out! Everywhere!

Linda We're in here, Geoffrey! We're in here!

Sound of gunfire. Closer.
Lights snap on. Linda, Joseph and Geoffrey in the room.

Are you / okay?

Joseph What are you seeing / out there?

Geoffrey There's no guard! The guy, he's gone! The gates are wide open! Where is everyone? What's going on? There are men coming down the street with machetes and clubs!

Joseph What is the uniform? Boy! What are / they wearing!

Geoffrey Nothing! There's no uniform! They're just – clothes – and –

Sound of smashing glass from offstage.

Jack (*offstage*) Jesus!

All turn as Jack enters.

Linda Jack! Are you all right? / What happened?

Jack Someone threw a rock through the – it almost hit me in the head!

Joseph (*to Geoffrey*) Where is your friend?

All look at Geoffrey.

Where is your friend, Geoffrey?

Sound of gunfire. Closer.

Geoffrey Gérard was with me. Isn't he here?

Joseph Pick up the phone, Jack. Please, pick up the phone. You are an American citizen. Please, Jack. Now.

Jack goes to the phone, picks it up. The phone is dead. He tries to make it work.

Jack Damn it damn it damn it / damn it damn it damn it damn it!

Joseph (*to Geoffrey*) What did you tell him? What does he know?

Bam. Bam.
  A knocking on the front door.
  Silence. No moves.
  Bam. Bam. Bam. Louder this time.
  No one moves.

Mizinga, the Man from the embassy party, and Gérard enter. The Man holds a rifle. Mizinga and Gérard hold machetes.

Mizinga Good evening.

No one moves.

Dr Exley. Linda.

Linda (*pause*) Samuel.

Joseph (*in Kinyarwanda*) Niko mwa bagabo mwe, ndabona twibeshye, reka mbere ke uko – [*Gentlemen, there's obviously been some sort of mistake. If you'll allow me to –*]

Man (*at Joseph in Kinyarwanda*) Ziba, wa cyitso we! [*Silence, Icyitso!*]

Mizinga I am sorry to disturb your evening. Tonight there is trouble all over Kigali. We are doing all we can to protect those who need to be protected. And our friends.

Pause.

Linda Thank you, that's / . . . thank you.

Jack We're fine. No need. Really.

Mizinga The patriot Martin Bucyana has been killed.

Joseph is visibly shaken. Jack and Linda look at each other.

Jack . . . I'm sorry, we don't / know who . . .

Mizinga A man who kept his country here, in his heart. Whose life has now been taken by terrorists. Tonight, all over this city, there will be a reckoning. We will take what we have come for, and we will not disturb you any longer.

No one moves.

Jack This man is our guest.

Man (*in Kinyarwanda*) Uwuhe muntu? / Ntamuntu mbona nyenzi gusa mbona hano. Umugambanyi ufite amaraso y'uburozi. Mbwira, mugihugu cyanyu, inyenzi muzikoza icyi?

Mizinga (*translating*) 'What man? I see no man. This is only a cockroach here. A traitor whose blood is poison. Tell me, in your country, what do *you* do with cockroaches?' I am only translating, you understand.

Jack This is our home.

Mizinga Yes. It was my pleasure to find it for you.

Jack I am asking you to leave.

Mizinga This is not your business. It does not concern you. (*turning to look at Linda*) I am sorry your eyes could not be opened, Linda. I apologise for my failure.

Jack No one is leaving.

Linda Jack, don't –

Jack (*to Linda, not looking at her*) Shut. Up. (*to Mizinga*) What are you going to do? Shoot us? You think you can just shoot us? Do you have any idea what would happen if –

Mizinga Please. Of course not. But this is a wanted man. A killer of Hutu children. I cannot be responsible for the people outside this house. What they will do if I were to leave without him. Let us not try that. No one wishes for that.

Linda (*to Mizinga*) We have lists. Names of people. You can have them. / Just leave. Please. Take them and –

Jack Linda! No! For God's sake! Don't say another –

Linda (*to Jack*) WE DO NOT BELONG HERE! THIS IS NOT OUR PROBLEM!

Mizinga Thank you, but that is not necessary. Do not worry about the lists. We have lists of every single cockroach in this nation. And one day soon, we will start hunting cabbages.

Joseph (*to Mizinga in Kinyarwanda*) Nyabuna, ndabinginze! Bararengana, ntacyobakoze! [*Please! I beg you! These are innocent people! They have done nothing!*]

The Man steps forward, cocks his rifle and aims it at Geoffrey's head. Geoffrey falls on his hands and knees. Jack tries to lunge towards him but Joseph steps in the way, grabbing him.
All overlapping:

Joseph / Jack! They are bluffing! They would never do it! Don't let them –

Jack / Please! Please don't! Please!

Linda / Oh my God oh my God oh my God oh my God.

Geoffrey Dad! Dad! Don't let them! Please! Don't let them – (*over everything*) DADDY!

Jack thrusts Joseph off him.

Jack (*to Mizinga, pointing at Joseph*) TAKE HIM!
TAKE HIM!
TAKE HIM!

No one moves.

Take him. Please.

Silence.
The Man with the rifle steps back next to Mizinga. He slowly rotates his gun until it is trained on Joseph. Gérard, machete in hand, crosses to Joseph and grips him.

Geoffrey is still on his knees. Jack goes to him.
Linda starts to go to Jack and Geoffrey, then stops.
No one moves.

Mizinga This will mean nothing to you soon. All of us, we will mean nothing. This is so unimportant to you. You will go home and forget. How fortunate you are.

The lights dim on the room. Bodies in tableau.
A light on Joseph, who turns and speaks to us.

Joseph We say here, Jack, that every day God strides the earth, but at night he returns always to sleep in Rwanda. He has given us so much. It is hard sometimes to dwell on what we have done with those gifts. The past here is an argument; the future, unknown. But today, in the present . . . I have hope.

Your true friend, Joseph Gasana.

The lights fade to darkness.

End of play.

Rwanda – 'Never Again'

FERGAL KEANE

*Fergal Keane covered the Rwandan genocide
for BBC News*

I have some good friends in the village of Nyarubuye in
south-east Rwanda on the border with Tanzania. It is a
remote place, several miles up a dirt track in the stony
hills overlooking the Akagera river and the East African
savannah. The person who is closest to me is a twenty-
year-old girl named Valentina who survived the Rwandan
genocide by hiding amid the bodies of her murdered
family and friends. They were murdered by her Hutu
neighbours and local police and soldiers acting on the
orders of the Mayor.

In the year before the catastrophe she was a teenage girl
hoping to move from her village school to a good
secondary education. I use the conditional advisedly. As
a Tutsi, Valentina was not guaranteed a proper education.
She belonged to a minority that had been discriminated
against and brutalised since Rwanda gained independence
from Belgium in the early 1960s.

Tutsis were shut out of any meaningful role in the
government, denied places at university, excluded from
the Civil Service. There were exceptions, but the general
picture was grim. After the Tutsi-dominated rebel
movement, the Rwandan Patriotic Front, invaded in
1990, attempting to force the government into a more
democratic dispensation, the level of oppression against
Tutsis increased dramatically.

As Hutu extremism became the dominant political
ideology so too did the idea of a great extermination gain

credence as the answer to the 'Tutsi problem'. Genocide became state policy. While the President talked peace with the rebels, his acolytes trained a militia to destroy the minority. All of the organs of state were harnessed to this end, most notably the security forces and the media. Radio and newspapers demonised the Tutsi. For some, the ruling elite's Tutsi-hating did not go far enough. Extremist opposition parties grew up with their own radio station and newspapers and their own militia.

In the daily life of Nyarubuye, a community of peasant farmers and cattle-herders, a place far from the city, it would have been difficult to detect just how dramatically the situation was changing in the early months of 1994. The local Tutsis had heard the radio broadcasts and noticed the militia being trained. The older ones would have experienced pogroms in 1959, again in the 1960s and also in 1973. But none expected a calamity on the scale of what was being planned by the extremists who now controlled Rwanda.

Valentina does remember that in the months before the genocide the atmosphere in her village began to change. Her parents tried to protect her from the poison being spread on the radio. But Hutu children at school began to make nasty remarks. The word 'foreigner' was being used to denigrate the Tutsi. There were mocking comments about people with long noses and fingers. (Hutu extremists claimed that the Tutsi were invaders who had come from the Horn of Africa centuries before.) Worst of all the Hutu teachers were indoctrinating their pupils with anti-Tutsi poison, singling out children like Valentina every time they taught Rwandan history.

The French historian of the genocide, Gérard Prunier, has a wonderful phrase to describe Rwanda in the months leading up to the explosion of violence. Rwanda, he writes, was 'a claustrophobic, airless hell'. A small elite, determined to preserve its power, was manipulating resentment into hatred, feeding on the fear of the Tutsi rebels, telling the Hutu they would be enslaved once more as in the old days when Belgian colonialists used Tutsi aristocrats to enforce their rule. In this tiny country, where Hutu and Tutsi lived crowded together on the green hills, the hatred was spreading like fire. The UN force that had been deployed to monitor a supposed peace and transition to a kind of democratic politics could see what was happening. But the warnings sent to New York, the appeal for a tougher approach to the extremists, went ignored by the high officials of the organisation. As the spring approached and incidents of violence increased, the architects of Rwanda's apocalypse simply waited for their moment.

When it came, on 6 April, with the shooting down of President Habyarimana's plane as it approached Kigali airport, the speed of the killing stunned the small UN force. By the time the genocide ended on 4 July some 800,000 people had been murdered by machete, axe, gun and grenade. In Nyarubuye, Valentina fled with her family to the local church. Within days it was surrounded and attacked by her Hutu neighbours. She watched as boys she had grown up with in the village hacked her loved ones to death.

Journalists have told some of the story of Rwanda. So too have historians. But I know that theatre can reach an audience, and convey truths, with a power that can elude those of us who operate in the strict language of the news bulletin or the newspaper dispatch. This play deals with Rwanda as it was in the early months of 1994, perched on the edge of the volcano. It was a time when the world knew very little of Rwanda or of the lives of children like Valentina. A play can entertain, challenge, upset and anger an audience; at its best it can make them think deeply about the world in which they live and be prepared to challenge orthodoxies and lies. This play is a powerful antidote to the kind of indifference which characterised our response to Rwanda. It is a call to action for those who care about the horrors currently being perpetrated against innocent people in Darfur, a reminder that if you believe in the words 'never again' you cannot simply leave the theatre feeling moved and inspired and allow those feelings to dissipate. Involve yourself in the fight for human rights. There are plenty of good organisations, like Human Rights Watch and Amnesty International, whose existence is our best hope of preventing another Rwanda. It really is *our* responsibility.

© Fergal Keane
May 2006

'Just Words'

*from interviews conducted in Rwanda and London
by J T Rogers and Max Stafford-Clark, February 2006*

WE WERE LIVING ALWAYS IN FEAR

We Tutsi were given names of insects, animals, viruses,
snakes. If you are constantly told this, subconsciously
you start to believe. You start to feel less than a human
being. There was an intellectual genocide before the
physical one. Tutsis were shut out of all important jobs.
In a Tutsi family, only the weakest one was allowed to
continue on in school. Tutsi were scapegoats, when
politicians needed scapegoats. A common enemy is easy:
all will be on your side. This is much easier than a
political solution. As the RPF [Rwandan Patriotic Front]
formed, then attacked, Hutus here said: 'If we had killed
all the Tutsis before, we wouldn't have these problems
now!' Yes, the Hutus chanted 'Tuzabat sembat semba!' –
'We will exterminate them!' – in the streets, but we thought
it was just words.

Jean Gakwandi, director of Solace Ministries

I was a doctor for five years at Kigali hospital. In October
1990, the weekend of the RPF's first attack, during
the bombing, we had to operate all night on patients
without anaesthetics. It was very hard. At the end of it,
my colleague turned to me and said, 'What is
Habyarimana waiting for? If he says kill Tutsis, I will –
starting with you!'

Senator Odette Nyiramilimo

The Interahamwe used to run practice drills in front of
the CND [Parliament building] to intimidate us. They

would hurl insults. There was talk of killing people, but nothing like genocide. We had studied history, but we were taken by surprise by the extent of the killings.

General Charles Kayonga,
commander of the RPF troops stationed
in the CND before and during the genocide

I thought when it finally came, they would kill the politicians. But not one million people. Not women and babies!

Jean-Pierre Sagahutu

LOOK, THE TRUTH IS MESSY

You can hardly differentiate between Tutsi and Hutu. I myself can barely tell. That's why they had identity cards! Just as I can't differentiate Europeans – French? English? Italian? That's why, during the genocide, very many Hutu died. Someone is tall, they are comparing noses. They see you, and you are killed. And yet maybe you are a Hutu.

Vénuste Karasira

We speak the same languages, we live in the same villages. Tutsis are tall and thin? Look at me, I am not tall or thin! Even ourselves, we are lost determining who is what.

Dr Vincent Biruta, President of Rwanda's Senate

Look, the truth is messy. The truth is that most Hutus were perpetrators *and* bystanders *and* protectors – it all depended on the day, and the situation. Every Hutu was involved in every part of the genocide. Every one. They had no choice, not if they wanted to live.

Anonymous

IT WAS SYSTEMATIC

It was systematic. Taxi drivers killed taxi drivers, doctors killed doctors. All knew each other here. Colleagues killed colleagues. My father was a doctor. Another doctor killed him.

Jean-Pierre Sagahutu

Those who organised the genocide used the tool of using everybody. If everyone is guilty, there is impunity. At the end of the day, who are you going to punish?

Geoffrey Ngiruwonsanga,
Programme Manager, The Survivors' Fund

People were told, kill as many as possible. Whatever you kill, you occupy. This is why there was massive participation with the poor people. It was like a competition.

Vénuste Karasira

THEY CUT LIKE THEY WERE CUTTING FLOWERS

My husband was killed on the night of 7 April 1994. My mother and two children were killed. My children were burned alive. I was alone with my nine-month-old. Killers found me hiding. 'Come, we will help you,' they said. Then they raped me. No one would help me. I was an animal in front of them . . . I was alone on the road for three days. I could not walk. A man came by and said, 'You will die, not with a gun but painfully.' He took me home and passed the time raping me. In the morning he took my baby, he took him to a big tree and beat his head, here and here, then hung him by the feet. Then he let him down, but he was already dead. I was made to dig the grave. After three weeks' walking at night, to find relatives. No food. No water. When I got there they were all dead. I lay down and slept for three days. Kids fetching water found me and said 'Oh, here is an old woman,' but I was twenty-three. I had spent three weeks looking for death but I had not found it. By my looks everyone feared to come near me . . . I was white. They thought I was a spirit.

Sarafina

The day the president's plane was shot down, young people came to my house. 'You people killed our president and we will kill you.' But we thought it was a joke, a mockery. These were our neighbours. My husband said, we are safe; they will not kill. A group of Interahamwe came and they cut like they were cutting flowers. My husband and five of my children were lain on the ground, in a line, and they were killed.

Agnes

During the genocide my family was killed and I was raped and kept as a sex slave for four weeks by a gang of Interahamwe. I was lucky that I was taken by one who was strong and not shared by five or twenty. I was locked in a house all day while they were out killing, then they came home and I would be raped. I never knew if I would be killed too. We had a family of not less than a thousand people. The whole village was made up of my family. Today there are only fifteen.

Margarita

I've been places with malevolent forces – people – before, but here it felt like the moral energy of the place had been sucked out and nothing had replaced it. It really felt like right was wrong and wrong was right. You could *hear* the leaves whispering – very bad things. All your senses were attenuated. The first day was very difficult. Dead people wherever you went: ditches, banana groves, schools. You walked into a school and saw piles of bodies. Houses of murdered Tutsi were entirely stripped, down to the wiring. Almost like soldier ants going through a body. It was medieval, really. Inexplicable. At a church we saw, I kept imagining God sitting on the roof, looking down on the bedlam. And then I imagined the Devil was there with him, dancing gleefully. 'Look at what I'm doing!'

David Belton, former journalist
and producer of the film Shooting Dogs,
interviewed in London

I was in hiding for two months and sixteen days, in an empty septic tank in Nyamirambo. I lost forty kilos. I came out only at two a.m., to try and find food and to stretch. I spent the days and nights hunched over, unable to move or stand. It was always loud, from the killings. Finally, one day it was so quiet I came out during the day. I saw soldiers and knew I was going to die. So I shouted at them, taunting them so that they would become so angry they would shoot me quickly and not cut me slowly with machetes. But they were not the government soldiers, they were RPF. I did not know the war was over.

Jean-Pierre Sagahutu

I dreaded going back, but I *had* to go back. This was June, after a month away. The country was empty. We flew to Goma and got there just ahead of a column of two million people who came through a corridor the size of this room, non-stop for two days. They were terrifying and dangerous: a beaten army who *knew* what they had done. I know they knew because I asked them.

David Belton

I HAVE NOT TOLD ANYONE THIS

Forty per cent of the women survivors were raped during the genocide. It was organised, a tool. Deliberate, this infection of HIV. Only peasant women will admit to being raped. Wealthier women, they won't talk about it. In our culture, we don't talk about sex, even forced sex. It's a taboo. They are ashamed to ask for help. If they do seek counselling, they end up seeing their tormentors. They go, they stand in a line – the same line with the men who raped them, or those men's wives. The survivor says, 'I would rather go hungry and die than stand with these people.'

Gabo Wilson, SURF Rwanda country director

There is a phenomenon here of survivors' guilt among the Tutsi who lived through the killings. Especially among women who were not raped or disfigured. This feeling that they got off easy, that they wish, in a twisted way, that they *had* been raped. One of the saddest things I've ever seen.

Helen Vesperini, Agence France-Presse

I had a child by my rapist. Working here, being helped by social workers, this is what taught me finally to love my child for the first time. This is why I have trained and become a social worker myself. But I have just tested positive for HIV. I am trying to be strong, but deep in my heart of hearts, I am asking – Why? Why? Why? I am told my child tested negative, but I think the doctors only told me that because they felt sorry. I have not told anyone else this. I cannot tell my family because I am supporting all of them. If they knew, they would lose all hope and sunlight. I have always liked acting and always wanted to be an actor. This is why I am telling you this. The theatre is important for this – to tell this.

Margarita

THE VICTIMS WILL NEVER FORGET

I live here with my sisters Beatrice and Joseanne. I am the head of the family. Our parents were killed in 1994. During the genocide. They were thrown in a lake. We saw this. I exchanged my life for my sisters', so they could have a better life. I take care of the gardens and try to make sure there is food to eat when my sisters come back from school. I till the land, I sell soap and salt. It was very hard at first to become used to all the responsibility. At first we had no money. I was selling tomatoes, and people were buying them not because they wanted tomatoes but because they were supporting me. My sisters may not appreciate what I do, but they do not

have a problem with it either. When they finish school,
I think they will help me to learn a trade and be a tailor.

Drocella Nyiraneza, aged twenty-two

What we are seeking is a repatriation of memory. We are
testimony that the genocide happened. There is no way
we live the way we do without a genocide. The victims
will never forget. The more you think and talk about it,
there is a slow healing. If not, it will just erupt.

Odette Kayirere, Coordinatrice Région Est,
Association des Veuves du Génocide Agahozo

A FIRE UNDERGROUND

I'm sorry I keep looking over my shoulder before
answering your questions. It's a habit we have here.

Anonymous

I was there. This 800,000 – this is not true. 400,000, at
most. This is how many that died. The RPF took my
country only to take the Congo. Where is the talk of
that? It is all about money and power; they had to get to
the Congo, as Rwanda has nothing. This is what you
must understand: it was a war, not a genocide. All these
dead bodies lying around after the war was over – tell
me, who would leave their families like that? Not bury
them like that? This was a plot. These bodies were placed
there. Propaganda. It is very simple: the RPF wanted
wealth. They passed as Hutus to do this killing. The Tutsi
are clever. Please do not say that I said this.

A Hutu survivor, interviewed in London

These killers convicted and imprisoned in Arusha, with
their so-called human rights. They have internet! They
have everything! It is just that they are not with their
families. Otherwise, they are okay.

A genocide survivor

So my question is, how do you get past it, when every street is framed with communal bloodletting? This wasn't Jews being secreted off to be gassed in Poland – it was all in plain sight.

David Belton

Could it happen here again? I don't think so. It was the Hutu Power leadership that supported all that. This government of reconciliation gives us hope. Once the older generation passes, once we are all gone, I believe Hutu and Tutsi will be a problem of the past.

A survivor

Now it is two hundred per cent safe here. But until when, I don't know. Rwanda is like a fire underground: the killings will come again.

Another survivor

It happened, therefore it can happen again:
this is the core of what we have to say.
It can happen, and it can happen anywhere.

Primo Levi, in *The Drowned and the Saved*